Cambridge Academic English

An integrated skills course for EAP

Teacher's Book

Intermediate

Anthony Manning, Chris Sowton, Craig Thaine

Course consultant: Michael McCarthy

CAMBRIDGE
UNIVERSITY PRESS

D1355011

CAMBRIDGE UNIVERSITY PRESS
Cambridge, New York, Melbourne, Madrid, Cape Town,
Singapore, São Paulo, Delhi, Mexico City

Cambridge University Press
The Edinburgh Building, Cambridge CB2 8RU, UK

www.cambridge.org
Information on this title: www.cambridge.org/9780521165259

First published 2012
Reprinted 2013

Printed in the United Kingdom by Latimer Trend

A catalogue record for this publication is available from the British Library

ISBN 978-0-521-165198 Student's Book
ISBN 978-0-521-165259 Teacher's Book
ISBN 978-0-521-165228 Class Audio CD
ISBN 978-0-521-165280 DVD
ISBN 978-1-107-607132 Class Audio CD and DVD pack

Contents

Introduction

Who is the course for?

Cambridge Academic English is for any student who needs English for their academic studies.

It is an integrated skills course, which means that, at each of the levels, students will develop their abilities in reading, writing, listening and speaking in an academic context. In your classes, there will probably be students studying or hoping to go on to study many different subjects. With this in mind, *Cambridge Academic English* includes topics and texts that will be of interest to students working in all subjects. However, some parts of the course also help students to develop abilities relevant to their particular area of study.

Using the Teacher's Book

The main intention of this Teacher's Book is to enable teachers to use the Student's Book in the best way possible. The notes have been organised in such a way that they can act as a guide for inexperienced teachers or teachers whose first language is not English, as well as a supplement and reference point for more experienced EAP practitioners. A wide range of information is included in the book, focusing in particular on the following areas.

Optional activities, which can help extend and clarify important areas.

Specific teaching strategies and procedures which correspond with the Student's Book activities.

Recommended interactions or groupings for particular activities.

Full and detailed answer keys.

Listening and speaking

7 Introducing your presentation

7.1 **Optional lead-in**

Ask students to brainstorm the kind of information which they would expect in the introduction of a presentation (e.g. overview of main topics, general background information, rationale, importance of topic).

a 👥 Students look at slides A and B and predict which words go in the spaces.

b Play ◀)1.2.

A types of taxation
B voting systems

Language note

The following language features are generally acceptable in presentations, but less so in academic writing:
– use of *I* (*here I'll focus on*)
– use of present continuous to outline ideas (*I'm going to highlight*)
– contractions (*That's*)
– cleft sentences (*What's meant by this is …*)
– rhetorical questions (*Why is this important?*)

Grammar and language notes which provide detailed information about difficult items and references to common learner errors, which can help you answer specific queries which may arise in the classroom.

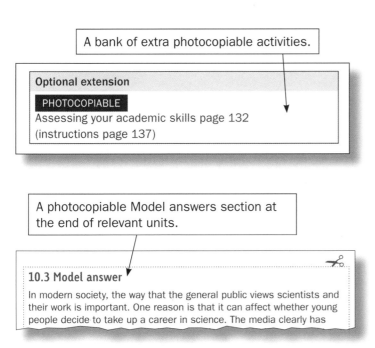

A bank of extra photocopiable activities.

Optional extension

`PHOTOCOPIABLE`

Assessing your academic skills page 132
(instructions page 137)

A photocopiable Model answers section at the end of relevant units.

10.3 Model answer

In modern society, the way that the general public views scientists and their work is important. One reason is that it can affect whether young people decide to take up a career in science. The media clearly has

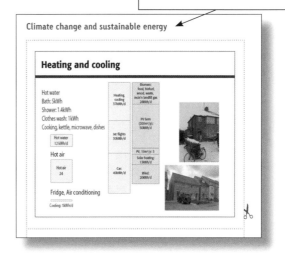

Photocopiable slides to accompany each lecture on the DVD-ROM.

What kind of language does the course teach?

Cambridge Academic English uses authentic academic English texts. The texts students will read are taken from the kinds of textbooks and journal articles that they might be recommended to read by their subject tutors. Students may find these challenging at first, but they will learn strategies in the course to help them cope. We believe that working with authentic texts in EAP is the best way of preparing to read them during students' academic course of study.

The lectures students will watch are delivered by experienced lecturers and researchers. In many colleges and universities around the world, students will be taught in English by some tutors who are native English speakers and others who are non-native English speakers. To help students prepare for this, both native and non-native English-speaking lecturers have been included in this course.

The vocabulary focused on in the course has been selected as being of particular importance in academic writing, reading, lectures and seminars. In choosing what to teach, we have made use of the Academic Word List compiled by Averil Coxhead (see www.victoria.ac.nz/lals/resources/academicwordlist for more information). This list includes many of the words that students are likely to meet in their academic studies.

To make sure that the language we teach in the course is authentic, we have made extensive use of the Cambridge Academic English Corpus (CAEC) in preparing the material.

⊙ What is the Cambridge Academic English Corpus?

The CAEC is a collection of 400 million words comprising two parts. One is a collection of written academic language taken from textbooks and journals written in both British and American English. The second is a collection of spoken language from academic lectures and seminars. In both parts of the corpus, a wide variety of academic subject areas is covered. In addition to the CAEC, we have looked at language from a 1.7 million word corpus of scripts written by students taking the IELTS test.

Conducting our research using these corpora has allowed us to learn more about academic language in use, and also about the common errors made by students when using academic English. Using this information, we can be sure that the material in this course is built on sound evidence of how English is used in a wide variety of academic contexts. We use the CAEC to provide authentic examples of how language is used, and to give you useful facts about how often and in what contexts certain words and phrases are used in academic writing.

Academic orientation

> **Aims**
> - Setting study goals in academic English
> - Focusing on academic study
> - Reading and writing in academic English
> - Attending lectures
> - Studying independently on an academic English course
> - Thinking about the role of language in academic English

1 Setting study goals in academic English

> **Optional lead-in**
>
> Explain to students that the aim of this unit is to train them how to use the rest of the book and to provide an introduction to academic English in use. You could ask students to introduce themselves, if this is the first class, and to describe any experience they have to date in learning English for Academic Purposes. As an extension, ask students to share with the class additional information regarding their current study purposes. You could ask them what they are working towards, and what their personal as well as institutional motivation is.

1.1 Give students ten minutes for this activity. Answers will vary according to each student's specific objective, and it may be useful to check the local progression requirements in your own institution in case students are hoping to move on to particular subject areas and don't quite understand what the requirements are. Progression targets can often be different according to subject, so it is worthwhile researching your class needs before you start.

1.2 👥 Students work in pairs to discuss questions 1–4. Encourage them to mix with others in the group and, if necessary, create new pairs by asking students to move around.

> **Optional extension**
>
> To encourage interactivity, ask each individual to explain to the class about their partner's study goals, rather than their own.

1.3 👥 Ask students to work in small groups for this exercise and, when they feed back, complete a table on the board listing their different responses.

> Suggested answers
>
> | Skill | Academic English |
> | --- | --- |
> | Reading | Longer texts on more specific and technical topics |
> | Writing | Formal writing such as essays and reports |
> | Listening | Listening to lectures and seminar discussions |
> | Speaking | Participating in seminars and debates |

2 Focusing on academic study

2.1a | **Optional lead-in**

> Ask students to discuss what their expectations are about studying overseas and what the differences are likely to be. If anyone has already studied overseas or had a holiday in another country, ask them to discuss how their expectations may have been different from the reality. Similarly, ask students to think about how they felt when they moved from primary school to secondary school, and to consider if there might be any parallels to draw between that experience and studying overseas for the first time.

👥 Encourage students to discuss the possible answers for this section in pairs. Suggest that they can draw on knowledge passed on from friends or relatives where possible.

> Suggested answers
> 1 12–15, depending on the course and institution
> 2 No, you'll need to conduct your own private study and research.
> 3 You'll get help through seminars and surgery hours, but often you'll have to ask if you need further clarification.
> 4 Often students are recommended to do two to three hours of private study for every hour spent in the classroom or lecture theatre.
> 5 Yes, it is very important to have good motivation, because if a student is not self-driven, it will be difficult to maintain enthusiasm for study.

2.1b After students have discussed their answers, play recording ◀0.1 and ask them to list the answers provided by Fei, noting any key similarities and differences. Encourage students to point out what they found most interesting or surprising about what he said.

2.2a This next section relates to reading, so it will be useful to start by asking students to discuss their current reading habits in their own language. How much do they currently read? What do they currently read? How do they feel about the idea of academic reading in English?

Answers will vary from student to student. However, it is useful to stress that reading is a crucial part of academic study, and that most students underestimate how much they are required to read.

2.2b 👥 Play recording ◀0.2. Encourage students to consider in pairs how their own views on reading may be similar to or different from those held by Christoffer.

3 Reading and writing in academic English

3.1a 👥 Organise students into groups of three. Encourage the groups to work through each key term and to explain why it relates to either reading or writing.

> 1 writing (in lectures)
> 2 reading/writing (in a text or an essay)
> 3 reading/writing (by an author or by you in an essay)
> 4 reading
> 5 This is the irrelevant term. It is most commonly associated with speaking.
> 6 reading (evaluating different arguments)
> 7 writing

3.1b Encourage students to fill the gaps in the summary by understanding the vocabulary in the box provided, and also by looking at the words on either side of the gaps in the summary. This is a useful way of using all the clues available.

> 1 find out
> 2 information
> 3 analyse

3.2a
> 1 topic
> 2 obvious
> 3 organise

Optional extension

Once students have correctly completed both of the summaries using the missing words, ask them to discuss the points made and to consider if there are any views expressed that they were not previously aware of. This could be an interesting and useful point for further debate if there are any key areas of disagreement. Differing opinions are particularly likely to arise if students have experience of a range of educational cultures.

3.2b 👥 / 👥 This activity invites students to draw further on their previous educational experience. If you have a range of different nationalities in the group, it will be useful to make pairs or groups which contain different nationalities.

4 Attending lectures

4.1

Optional lead-in

Ask students to think about any experience that they might have of attending lectures and to think about the challenges they encountered. If they haven't yet attended lectures, ask them to consider what the most demanding aspects of learning in this way might be.

Once students have worked through the questions and discussed which are helpful and which are not, ask them to justify their answers. Where necessary, use your professional judgment to provide guidance if students aren't able to see the merit in some of the helpful ideas.

> 1 helpful
> 2 not helpful
> 3 not helpful
> 4 not helpful
> 5 helpful
> 6 not helpful

4.2 This activity is an exercise in listening for specific information; explain to students that this is one key aspect of listening to lectures. Once students have listened to Maria in recording ◀0.3, ask individuals to point out the suggestions that overlap with those in **4.1**.

4.3 👥 Divide the class into groups of three and appoint one individual in each group as the scribe. Invite groups to discuss each study resource in turn. At the end, when the table is complete, the scribe can present the results to the rest of the class.

Suggested answers

Study resource	How can we use this resource?
Pre-lecture reading texts	To help prepare yourself and develop an initial understanding of the topic
Your notes	To develop your synthesis of the main points made
Other students	To clarify meaning and your understanding

5 Studying independently on an academic English course

Optional lead-in

As this section focuses on independent learning, ask students how their previous study at school has prepared them for independent learning. Ask them to clarify what they think independent learning is, and why it is important.

5.1
b speaking
c reading
d writing
e vocabulary
f listening

Ask students to discuss which of these ideas they have existing experience of.

5.2 Make a list on the board of any extra useful ideas which students suggest, and encourage them to take notes so that they can use these recommendations for their own future purposes. In a couple of weeks' time, you could revisit this list and ask students if they have managed to put these suggestions into practice.

Optional extension

PHOTOCOPIABLE

Discussing problems and identifying solutions
page 110 (instructions page 103)

6 Thinking about the role of language in academic English

6.1 👤 / 👥 Ask students to read the text individually and then to discuss the question in pairs. Encourage students not to use a dictionary and to focus on the main meaning of the text.

The text points out that it is also important to know how to use grammar and vocabulary in the context of academic writing.

6.2 This is a really useful initial diagnostic test. Try to observe which students are familiar with the terminology and are able to identify the matching examples. Your observations of the class will help to identify some of their areas of strength and weakness.

2 verb – *practise*
3 adjective – *important*
4 adverb – *clearly*
5 pronoun – *it*
6 preposition – *from*
7 prefix – *mis-*
8 suffix – *-ly*
9 collocation – *aspects of*

Optional extension

Encourage students to revise any of the terms that they were not familiar with in this exercise and to be prepared for a quick informal class test in the next session.

1 Styles of learning

Getting started

1 How do you learn?

1.1

Optional lead-in

To introduce this topic, ask students to think about their experience of studying and learning at schools and colleges in their home country and their time studying overseas. Ask them how many different institutions (e.g. kindergarten, primary school, secondary school, Sunday school) they have attended, and to list as many different things that they have learned (e.g. subjects and skills) as they can.

1 Books open. Ask students to think of answers to the questions about positive learning experiences and the reasons why they were positive. If they struggle to think of examples from school, encourage them to refer to learning experiences from their parents or from other activities. Ask individual class members to share their experiences with the rest of the class.

2 Move on from the more general discussion above and ask students more specifically about their experiences of writing essays in their first language. Ask them in which subjects they are most familiar with essay writing.

In pairs, students discuss their experiences of essay writing and how they normally approach an essay-writing task. What is the first thing they do, and what, if any, planning do they undertake? What have they been taught to do when writing an essay in their first language?

Note

Monolingual groups are likely to have shared experiences of the same cultural requirements of essay writing, if they come from a similar educational background. You can use this to gain a more detailed explanation of what characterises essay writing in that particular linguistic culture. Multilingual groups will be able to discuss a range of different experiences in essay writing and the priorities that are key in this form of communication across different regions of the world.

3 Ask students to think of studying as a global term and to break it down into the range of sub-activities that can be included within the term *studying*. You could use a spider diagram to initiate the process.

4 In order to lighten the topic of this activity, encourage students to think of the feedback that they may have received for their homework from teachers and tutors in their previous study experiences. This may help them to remember the kind of adjectives that have been used to describe students' study approach(es). Ask them to talk about any differences in the way they see themselves as learners, and the way in which teachers have perceived them in the past. For example, a tutor may previously have considered a student to be lazy in class, but actually this may be more about being shy.

5 First, ask students if they have previously given thought to the actual process of learning and how they can improve their own skills in this way.

The feedback for the second part of this question could be best collected by dividing the class into two groups. Ask students who prefer learning on their own to go to one side of the classroom and those who prefer group or team work to move to the other side. Then get each group to list reasons why they prefer that particular approach.

1.2a After the activity in **1.1** part 5, present students with both the summaries of this essay question and ask them to evaluate which is the correct answer. Try to get them to understand that the key lies in understanding your strengths and weaknesses as a student, rather than adopting any particular single approach to study. There are different circumstances when both working alone and teamwork are acceptable means of study or achieving something. Different situations may require different approaches.

> Summary 2

1.2b 👥 Before asking the group to decide on which essay type is best, divide the class into three groups and ask them to put together a definition and explanation of each of the types of essay listed. Use this opportunity to make sure that the class understands the different types of essay. Then ask the group to decide which essay type is most suitable for this particular title. Try to elicit a rationale that explains why the discursive essay is best suited (because it allows consideration and evaluation of differing perspectives; it is more critical in nature).

> Essay type 3 (also known as a discursive essay)

Reading

2 Reading for key terms and guessing meaning in context

2.1 In order for students to demonstrate their understanding of the terms *abstract* and *practical* in the essay title, ask them to give examples of things that can be described using these two adjectives.

2.2 After reading the extract, ask students to confirm if their understanding of the two terms has remained the same or developed further. Check any vocabulary that may not have been understood by all students.

2.3 Check students' understanding and have other members of the group explain if any of the suggested responses do not align with these answers.

> **1** abstract
> **2** practical
> **3** practical
> **4** practical
> **5** practical

2.4 Go through each of the words in turn and nominate a student to provide the correct response. Ask the class for a consensus agreement before revealing the answers. You could split the class into two or more teams for this and make it competitive by giving points for correct answers.

> **1** b   **2** a   **3** a

3 Grammar in context: *-ing* forms

3.1a 👤 / 👥 Ask one student or a pair to write the words which use *-ing* forms on the board. Next, using a dictionary, ask the class to find the *-ing* words and to identify the different kinds of word. Make the point that although *-ing* words may look the same, they are actually used in different situations as different parts of speech.

> **1** starting
> **2** learning, doing, trying, watching
> **3** guessing, meaning, learning
> **4** signing

3.1b Before completing this activity, ask students to present their findings from the dictionary work they did in **3.1a**. If they have used the dictionary properly, they should have made observations that will be similar to the answers to exercises in this section.

> **1** noun
> **2** nouns
> **3** noun; adjective
> **4** verb/present participle

Optional extension

Read these example sentences and decide if *abstract* is being used as a noun or an adjective.

– *She sent in the abstract for her conference presentation for the committee to consider.* (noun)
– *The reason why I don't want to continue studying philosophy is that I find the ideas too abstract and not connected with day-to-day life.* (adjective)
– *The benefit of abstract thinking is that you don't need to worry about practical details – it frees my mind.* (adjective)
– *I always read the abstracts of journal articles quite carefully because they tell me if the article is worth reading or not.* (noun)
– *I don't enjoy his tutorials. When I ask a question, his explanations are so abstract that I can't understand what he's saying and I end up feeling more confused.* (adjective)

3.2 Before reading and completing the rule in this section, ask students if they can suggest the rules themselves.

> **1** verbs   **2** adjectives   **3** nouns

4 Grammar in context: present simple in academic English

4.1 Write the two sentences on the board and ask students to come to the front of the class to highlight the present simple, as indicated in the question. In order to illustrate the usage for a) routine and habit in contrast to what is b) general occurrence, ask students to create similar sentences from their own experience. For example:

a) *The sun shines in the summer.*

b) *I go to bed at ten o'clock at night.*

| a | **1** learn | **2** study |
| **b** | routine/habit = 2 | generally true = 1 |

4.2 **Optional lead-in**

This section could be approached in a number of ways. As the aim is to identify further rules for the usage of the present simple, you may like to start by asking students to list any further rules that they are aware of.

👤 / 👥 / 👥👥 You could allocate different questions within the section to different groups, pairs or individuals and then gather feedback at the end. This would make a useful and interesting way of piecing together a set of rules.

a Function 2
b It's possible, but not necessary – both past simple and present simple can be used.
c 1 ✓   2 ✗   3 ✓

Note

See the Grammar and vocabulary section for further practice.

Listening and speaking

5 Asking for study help

5.1 🔊1.1 To prepare students for listening activities, it is always useful to set the scene by asking them to think about the context that they are about to listen to. This is a way of tuning in before the listening activity starts. In the real world, there are many contextual clues that help us understand what we are listening to, so it can be useful to re-create this in the classroom as far as possible. From the Student's Book, it is apparent that the conversation is set in a library and it is about working with colleagues. Focus students by asking some of these questions:

– *Do you enjoy team-working, or do you prefer working alone?*

– *What challenges do you think team-working presents?*

– *What kinds of resource can you find in a library?*

– *How do libraries work?*

– *What kind of work do you think Diana and Charlie will be doing in the library?*

1 She doesn't understand why he has to return a library book he only took out yesterday.
2 surprised
3 He didn't go to the library tutorial, so isn't sure how returning books works.

5.2 This next conversation takes place between a librarian and a student. Before playing the recording, ask students to think of what that conversation might involve. What questions would they ask each other? Then play recording 🔊1.2.

1 yes
2 Students have to return books if another student puts a reserve on them.

5.3 Play recording 🔊1.2 again. Encourage students to listen for detail by crossing off each of 1–5 when they hear them. The one item left uncrossed will then be the correct answer.

They do not do 2.

5.4 Ask students to look at the expressions. Is the speaker asking for permission or asking for information? Ask students to think of examples of sentences which perform each function. If they are not sure, provide some yourself and write them on the board. This will get them used to what they might expect to hear and will help them to identify the correct answer.

The speaker is asking for information in all of them.

5.5 Before playing the recording, read this sentence aloud, using intonation to emphasise the politeness of the question:

Can you tell me where the short-loan section is, please?

Then read the same sentence again without the emphasis on intonation. Ask students which sentence sounds more polite to them. Now play recording 🔊1.3 and ask students to identify the more polite form in each of the six pairs. When they have done this, get them to analyse what caused them to choose their answers. Finally, play recording 🔊1.4 with further examples of the same contrast for students to listen to and repeat.

a 1 a   2 b   3 b   4 a   5 b   6 a
b 2

5.6

Optional lead-in

Before practising the expressions, it might help to watch one of the videos available on YouTube. Just type 'university library' into the search engine. Alternatively, the video provided by De Montfort University on this topic is available at the following link: http://www.youtube.com/watch?v=jvoLfbmBpXE.

Practise the expressions from **5.4** in order to familiarise students with the university library environment.

If students are nervous about using the role-play cards, make sure they have enough time to plan what they are going to say.

👥 Go around the class and monitor students while they are practising, and choose a confident pair to perform in front of the class.

Reading

6   Scan reading

6.1   In preparation for this activity, encourage students to go to the library in their current institution and use the library computer to find a book. If necessary, give the class a single book title so that they find similar details in their search. Ask them to either print out or write down some of the information that they find. If they don't have access to a library with a computerised catalogue, they may be able to use a search engine such as Unicorn by logging on to a university website.

In the next class, ask them to show the results that they have gathered and the different types of information they have found.

> **2** the title of the book
> **3** the reference number on the book (call number)
> **4** information on if you can get the book
> **5** the place of publication
> **6** the publisher
> **7** the year of publication
> **8** the author

Optional extension

1 What do we call the reference number that tells you where to find the book in the library? (call number)

2 If the book is currently in the library and ready to borrow, what will the search result say? (available)

6.2   Depending on the time available, you may wish to divide these questions amongst two or three teams in the class or make it a competition with a prize for whoever can finish first. As a practice activity for this exercise, you could give the class a photocopy of the inside page of a book which contains this type of bibliographic information. Ask them to label the different type of information that is available. This may help them answer the questions in this section more quickly, as they will already recognise the kind of details that are displayed.

> **2** journal
> **3** *Learning styles in education and training*
> **4** 370.153TIL
> **5** *The Kolb learning style inventory*
> **6** no
> **7** *Learning for themselves: pathways to independence in the classroom*
> **8** an e-book

Optional extension

PHOTOCOPIABLE

Understanding book reviews page 111 (instructions page 103)

6.3   Scan reading is useful for locating specific words, phrases or numbers in texts without necessarily understanding the information around the word, phrase or number.

> **a** 2   **b** 3

6.4   Draw students' attention to the importance of *discuss*, which identifies which type of essay Diana will have to write.

> successful, discuss

6.5   Encourage students to examine each of the books in turn and not to be influenced by Diana's initial decision. Explain the importance of objectivity. Clarify the point that the aim is to identify books which may be relevant to the essay title. Make sure students are also aware that they shouldn't be put off by words in the book titles that they may not understand.

> All of Diana's decisions are good except for the ones relating to Book 2 and Journal 6. Not understanding a word or term is not a good reason not to look at a book, and the term *learning style* is in the title, so it is likely to be relevant. The journal *Learning and teaching* is not only going to be about teaching. Furthermore, it is a journal and will contain different articles, some of which will focus on learning and quite possibly on learning styles. It is therefore worth looking at this journal.

7 Reading for your course

Play recording ⏴1.5.

> 1 Maria and Fei mention compulsory reading lists. Maria contrasts this with 'books ... you could be interested in', while Fei mentions reading that is 'important for your study'.
> 2 Anitha did less reading because she was studying maths.

8 Gist reading

Optional lead-in

As a quick introduction to the term *learning styles*, ask students to look at the results from a set of Google definitions. You can get this by typing 'define: learning styles' into Google or by using the following link: http://www.google.co.uk/search?hl=en&q=define%3A+learning+styles+&meta=.

8.1 This question is a good measure of the gist-reading skills of the class. They should be able to answer this question if they have gathered some of the underlying meaning within the text.

> The descriptions refer to both abstract ideas and practical learning.

Optional extension

If you have time, there is also an interesting online learning-styles inventory which can be completed free on the Accelerated Learning website (http://www.acceleratedlearning.com/method/test_launch.html). This could be a worthwhile homework activity if there isn't time in class. This will help students to understand the nature of the text more fully before they start reading. It is also likely they will need some synonyms for the word *inventory*, which is likely to be unfamiliar to many of them.

8.2 | **1** no **2** yes **3** no **4** yes

8.3 Ask students to justify why they think they have a particular learning style and what they think are the strengths and weaknesses of that style.

Optional extension

If you had time to look at the inventory on the Accelerated Learning website (see **8.1** extension), ask students to compare the two inventories and the results. Ask students to explain why they think it is useful to understand your learning style in more depth.

Writing

9 Organising ideas

9.1 Make students aware that before something can be discussed, the nature of what is being discussed first needs to be explained, otherwise the discussion may be confused or off topic.

There isn't any point discussing something if you don't know what you're discussing!

The extract provided describes different learning styles. This is done first so that the usefulness of understanding learning styles in independent learning can then be discussed later.

> **a** The explanation should come first.
> **b** It's from the explanation.

Note

See the Grammar and vocabulary section for further practice

9.2 A general statement is provided at first in order to give an initial description of each of the styles. Further information is then given in order to give more detail, and this is finally summed up at the end of each section.

> Description 2

9.3
> **a 1** four (cardinal number)
> **2** four (cardinal number)
> **3** first (ordinal number)
> **4** second (ordinal number)
> **b 1** cardinal
> **2** ordinal

Optional extension

As a vocabulary-building exercise, ask students to think of adjectives associated with a number of the learning styles introduced in this unit. You could ask students to work in pairs or, if they are confident, to work alone. Give the class ten minutes' thinking time and then build up a series of spider diagrams on the board, showing each learning style in the centre and the adjectives around the outside.

10 Linking words 1

10.1 As an introduction, explain to students that linking words are used to connect ideas and sentences within a paragraph or essay. Ask them to list any linking words that they are already aware of. If students need further explanation, you can explain the different categories of linking expression and ask them to give examples such as these.

Adding details

and	in addition	as well as	also
too	furthermore	moreover	apart from
in addition to	besides	what is more	

Summing up

in brief	in short	in summary	to summarise
to put briefly	to conclude	in conclusion	to sum up
as a final point			

Organising ideas

the former … the latter	firstly, secondly, finally	the first point is	lastly
the following			

Providing a reason

due to / due to the fact that	owing to / owing to the fact that	because	because of
since	as	due to	as a result of
according to			

Contrasting

but	however	even though / although	despite / despite the fact that
on the other hand	nevertheless	nonetheless	while
whereas	in spite of / in spite of the fact that	by contrast	

1	according to
2	by contrast
3	although

10.2
1	four
2	first
3	A
4	By contrast
5	third
6	although

To test the depth of students' understanding, ask them to identify which category of linking expression in **10.1** each of the words in **10.2** falls into.

10.3 This exercise would make a good timed activity to finish off this section of the unit. Ask students to review the different exercises they have covered, and then to write the summary, incorporating some of the language that they have studied. Encourage them to move from general to more specific in their descriptions of the different 'layers', and to use connectives where possible and appropriate.

👤 / 👥 When students have finished this individually, ask them to compare their work in pairs. Go around and correct students' writing while they are discussing each other's work.

See the model answer on page 17.

Focus on your subject

Ask students to feed back to the class regarding some different categories within their own particular areas of academic specialism or interest. This is a useful way to show students the transferability of the language and skills studied in this unit.

Grammar and vocabulary

- Noun forms
- *-ing* forms
- Present simple in academic English
- Sentences with *if* that talk about what is generally true
- Collocations with *conclusion*

1   Noun forms

Optional lead-in

Introduce students to the idea of changing adjectives to nouns by using suffixes. First, test their knowledge of prefixes and suffixes, then ask them to decide which suffix will work for each of the groups in this table.

**Suffixes: (1) *-ment* (2) *-ness* (3) *-ity*
(4) *-ance, -ence* (5) *-ship* and *-hood***

1	2	3
replace	kind	possible
arrange	happy	complex
refresh	sad	pure
employ	dark	major
merry	weak	superior
4	**5**	
absent	relation	
silent	member	
important	bachelor	
relevant	child	
assistant	friend	

1a   **1** reflection   **2** association   **3** consciousness

1b   **1** reflection   **2** consciousness   **3** association

Optional extension

Ask students to practise using the dictionary to find the definitions listed in the Student's Book. If there is time, ask students to use the dictionaries to create a similar activity using three of the words in the above table and their definitions from the *CALD*.

1.2   As this section again refers to different parts of speech and ways of using suffixes to convert verbs to nouns, check that students are taking appropriate notes in a record book of some description. Make sure students are using a systematic method of logging how different vocabulary items can change their form through the use of different suffixes.

Stress that words like *silent, silently* and *silence* should not be logged three separate times, but recorded once with an understandable reference which shows how the different parts of speech are created.

Encourage students to bring their vocabulary books to every class and monitor the way in which they record new words and definitions.

Verb	Noun	Verb	Noun
1 anticipate	*anticipation*	**5** cooperate	*cooperation*
2 appreciate	*appreciation*	**6** exhibit	*exhibition*
3 aware	*awareness*	**7** isolate	*isolation*
4 construct	*construction*	**8** select	*selection*

1.3a

New word: *associate* (v)	
definition:	**5** to connect someone or something in your mind with someone or something else [CALD]
register:	**3** ~~formal~~ neutral ✓ ~~informal~~
pronunciation:	**1** /əˈsəʊsiːjeɪt/
word forms:	**2** association (n)
common collocations:	**4** noun form: *in association with*

1.3b

New word: *appreciate* (v)	
definition:	to recognise or understand that something is valuable, important or as described [CALD]
register:	~~formal~~ neutral ✓ ~~informal~~
pronunciation:	/əˈpriːʃijeɪt/
word forms:	appreciation (n) appreciative (adj)
common collocations:	verb form: *fully appreciate* noun form: appreciation *of/for*

Optional extension

Ask students to bring their vocabulary books to the next class and to follow the pattern described for recording new items. It may be useful to take in the vocabulary books and even mark them, in order to emphasise the importance of good record-keeping.

2 *-ing* forms

2.1
2 Making
3 find
4 thinking
5 studying; joining
6 debate
7 teaching; motivating
8 read; interesting

2.2
Making (n)   thinking (adj)   studying (v)   joining (v)
teaching (adj)   motivating (adj)   interesting (adj)

3 Present simple in academic English

3.1
✓ = correct, ✗ = incorrect
2 ✗ ~~suggests~~ suggest
3 ✗ ~~focus on~~ focuses on
4 ✓ argue
5 ✗ ~~identifies~~ identify
6 ✗ ~~shows~~ show
7 ✓ explains
8 ✗ ~~describe~~ describes

4 Sentences with *if* that talk about what is generally true

4.1
a Sentence 4
b a Sentences 4, 5   b Sentences 1, 2, 3

4.2
1 *if* + subject + <u>present</u> simple, subject + <u>will</u> + base form of verb
OR *if* + subject + <u>past</u> simple, subject + <u>would</u> + base form of verb
2 *if* + subject + <u>present</u> simple, subject + <u>present</u> simple
OR *if* + subject + <u>present</u> simple, subject + <u>may</u> + base form of verb

4.3
1 may find
2 find
3 won't
4 are
5 will be

4.4
1 If you don't do some reading before lectures, you will find them difficult to understand.
2 If you enrol and pay for the second semester now, you'll get a discount on your fees.
3 If you go to tutorials, you get a chance to discuss course content with other students.
4 If you talk to your lecturer, he'll let you know whether you can have an extension on your assignment.
5 If a student's motivation is strong, their learning style is not that important.

5 Collocations with *conclusion*

5.1
Definition 2

5.2
1 simple
2 the
3 second
4 easily
5 about

Model answer

10.3 Model answer

Curry describes a model of learning which consists of four different layers. The first layer is called the 'instruction preference' and describes the kind of learning context that learners prefer. The second layer is called 'social interaction'. This states that learners prefer to interact with other people when learning. A third layer is called 'information processing style'. This outlines the individual way learners understand information. The final layer is known as 'cognitive personality style' and describes the learner's personality which can be seen in different learning situations. Curry suggests that although the first layer is closest to the outside and can be changed, the fourth level, in the middle of the onion, is less flexible and difficult to change.

2 Problems in the natural world

Unit aims

READING
- Understanding essay questions
- Identifying the relevance of the text
- Grammar in context: noun phrases

LISTENING AND SPEAKING
- Making sure you have understood

WRITING
- Paragraph building
- Grammar in context: present perfect

Getting started

1 Living things and the environment

1.1 With books closed, introduce students to this topic area by asking them to focus on problems in the natural world that might be particularly relevant to their own countries or backgrounds. Ask each student to think of three problems. Students should create a spider diagram for each problem so that they can link it to any connected issues.

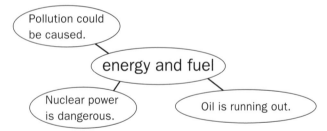

👤 / 👥 Once each student has identified a number of problems, divide them into pairs, preferably with a student from a different country or region. Ask students to explain each of the three problems that they have identified to their partner. Before they begin, ask each pair to think about *how* and *why* each of the problems has occurred. They could also think about *who* or *what* is *affected* or *influenced* by each of the problems.

Then ask them to focus on the aspects listed in the Student's Book.

1.2 Books open. Compare ideas with other students.

1.3 | Suggested answers
| biology, chemistry, biotechnology, agricultural science, environmental studies, veterinary science, geology, geophysics, landscape architecture

Reading

2 Understanding essay questions

2.1 | **Optional lead-in**
| Before looking at the essay title, focus students on the topic of 'problems in the natural world'. They can base this on their discussions in **1.1**, but in a broader context. Ask them to look at the different categories – human beings, animals, insects and plants – whilst considering both positive and negative effects that these creatures may have on the environment.

Ask students to use the *CALD* to find the words and their definitions. Test students' understanding further by getting them to list different types of organism and making sentences using the two words in an authentic manner.

| *organism* = single living thing, e.g. plant, animal, virus
| *ecosystem* = all living things and the way they affect each other and the environment
| Organisms are part of an ecosystem.

2.2a Explain to students that key words are the words which provide the main meaning for a particular text. They are the words that you really have to understand in order to follow the text properly. Some words are not so important and you can jump over them, provided that you understand the key words.

Ask students to use a coloured pen or a highlighter to mark the words in the essay title which they think are key. For stronger students, ask them to categorise the key words according to their relative importance. This could be done using different colours.

👤 / 👥 Ask individual students or pairs to discuss their findings and to agree on a single set of key words which need to be understood to follow the essay title. You can then write an agreed list of key words on the board by collecting ideas from the different pairs.

| Suggested answer
| <u>Living organisms</u> can play <u>important roles</u> in <u>ecosystems</u>. <u>Discuss</u> how an organism of <u>your choice</u> plays a <u>key role</u> in an ecosystem. <u>Show</u> how <u>human activity</u> has had an impact on both the organism and ecosystem.

2.2b 👥 Ask students to think about the purpose of each of the different sentences within the essay title. If possible, divide the class into three groups for this and ask each group to agree on the purpose of each of the three sentences.

> The first sentence outlines a general position or opinion. The other two sentences require a specific focus on one particular example that supports the general statement. It is important to understand that the essay should focus on the specific example, rather than extended discussion of the general thesis statement.

2.3 👥 Ask students to discuss in pairs the purpose of the words in each box. After five minutes' discussion, collect the feedback and reach a consensus with the rest of the class.

> **1** The words in Box B are key **instruction** words that tell students how to approach the essay title.
> **2** The words in Box A are key **content** words for the essay title. These will all need to be defined, exemplified and discussed.

Optional extension

PHOTOCOPIABLE

Instruction words and content words page 112 (instructions page 103).

2.4 This activity encourages students to understand what they need to do in the essay and provides a structured strategy for gaining assistance from their tutor. Explain how writing questions and then trying to find the answers can help to make the task of essay writing more achievable and manageable. This will help to show how essay writing is a step-by-step process, rather than one large global task.

To provide an example, ask students to think of the questions they might ask if they were told they were going to have a test tomorrow. Typically, they might ask some of these questions:

1 *How long will the test be?*

2 *What will the test focus on?*

3 *How many sections will the test have?*

4 *What type of questions will I have to answer?*

Explain that by finding answers to these questions and understanding the different individual elements, the task set can become more manageable and less worrying. The same process can be used to understand the process of preparing for an essay.

Make sure that students understand the importance of asking tutors for clarification when such essays or exercises are set.

> Suggested answers
> **1** No, the focus of the essay should be on one specific ecosystem.
> **2** The student should make the choice and not wait to be given a choice by her lecturer or tutor. The phrase 'your choice' is a key feature of this particular question; it means students need to make a decision about a specific living organism to focus on.
> **3** There will need to be some description/discussion of the organism in general, but most of the essay should include discussion of the organism in relation to the ecosystem.
> **4** Yes, so it means the student will need to choose an organism that is seen as being important in an ecosystem. In other words, there could be problems with the ecosystem.
> **5** No, it should be limited to the ecosystem that is being discussed in the essay.
> **6** Yes: it could be either or both.
> **7** The student should do both, but she needs to provide plenty of examples to support her argument.

2.5 In order to focus students on the process of essay-title analysis, write the title on the board. Tell the class you are going to show them how to start the first step in essay writing, and annotate the title as below.

The image shows each of the three parts of the title circled, with key words and instruction words underlined. There are also question marks next to words that need checking in the dictionary, and a further series of questions for consideration.

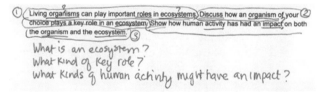

Once you have written this on the board, ask students to consider what the different notes indicate, and which processes have been followed.

> **a** B → E → D → A → C
> **b** Option 3

Listening and speaking

3 Making sure you have understood

3.1 👥 Students work in pairs to answer each of the questions. Encourage the class to draw on their previous expectations. Where possible, refer to the different roles within your particular department, as there are likely to be clear examples of different staff members with different areas of responsibility.

> **1 b + c**: Students can begin by asking classmates and sharing ideas. In most institutions, it would be acceptable to ask a tutor or lecturer.
>
> **2** Neither of the groups is likely to want to help with (a). Classmates will be busy thinking about the content of their own essays. However, classmates will probably help with (b) and (c). Tutors and lecturers are likely to help with only (b).

3.2

> **Optional lead-in**
>
> Before students start to listen, ask the whole class to suggest what they think the conversation may involve. This will focus them on the context and what the student may be asking the tutor. Even if they don't suggest exactly the same situation, it will be a useful way to start thinking about this kind of situation.

Play recording 🔊2.1 for students to listen to the conversation.

> **1** b   **2** bees

3.3 🔊2.2 Encourage students to look at the different sentence parts and to work out which parts fit together in order, before they listen and check their answers.

> **1** I just want to be sure that by 'living organism' the question means either insects or animals and not just animals.
> **2** So what exactly is meant by an 'ecosystem'?
> **3** So am I right in thinking that a fruit orchard could be an ecosystem?
> **4** Another thing I'd like to check is the meaning of the phrase 'key role'.
> **5** How important is the final part?

3.4 👤 / 👥 Ask students to try to identify why they have reached their decision. Why is it clear that Katya is checking information?

> **1** c
> **2 a** Example 3   **b** Example 2
> **3** a

For questions 2 and 3, ask students to give alternative example sentences to show that they understand how the words *so* and *just* can be used in these contexts.

3.5a Before students begin this activity, make sure they realise that the meaning of the original sentence does not need to change, and that the rewritten expressions will retain the same meaning. Ask students if they can remember what a synonym is, as this will help them to identify some of the words to use from the box.

> **1** I'**d like** to be **certain** that …
> **2** So am I **correct** in **believing** that …?
> **3** Another **point** I **just want** to check is …
> **4** How **necessary** is it to …?

3.5b 👥 Students work in pairs to find the matching halves of the sentences introduced in **3.5a**. Tell them first of all to think of how the sentences need to connect grammatically before thinking of the meaning.

For example, in sentence 1, they can guess that the word *that* needs to be followed by a personal pronoun, which will lead them immediately to matching the third option from the box.

> **1** … we have to use statistics.
> **2** … we have to use statistics.
> **3** … whether we have to use statistics.
> **4** … use statistics.

3.6 Ask students to stand up for this activity, as it is likely to help them to bring more energy to the dialogues. It would also be useful if they moved to a different corner of the classroom or worked with a different partner. Encourage them to relax as much as possible and, after preparing, not to read the text from any notes they may have made. This may help conversation to flow more naturally.

3.7 This could include any of the following: the kind of degree their partner wants to do; specific courses; English-language study goals (i.e. to get a specific IELTS score or pass some kind of exam). If weaker students are struggling to think of questions, ask them to list the different ways to start a question using *Wh-* and *How*. This will help them to think of the kinds of questions that they could pose.

Reading

4 Identifying the relevance of the text

4.1 Ask students to look at the photo and captions. Ask them to suggest reasons why honeybees might be important. This should help them to prepare for the text in **4.5**, and may help them to understand the context while they read.

Give the class five minutes to study the list of statements and get them to vote on whether the statements are true or false. Nominate students to explain why each of the answers is either true or false. Try to get them to provide evidence to support their answers where possible.

> **1** True
> **2** True: They do this by pollinating flowering plants.
> **3** False: Most bees live in communities, but some species live alone in nests they create for themselves.
> **4** False: There are no bees in Antarctica.
> **5** True

4.2 For this question, solicit suggestions from the class and write the ideas on the board in a brainstorm pattern. This will help prepare students for understanding the possible themes in the text. Accept any answer at this stage. The aim is just to get students thinking.

4.3 **2** transfer **3** another **4** means **5** can

4.4 Before students fill in the table, refer them to each of the missing words and ask them to decide which, out of a verb and a noun, is most likely to be considered as an action and whether, in the last row of the table, *the insect* would be considered a verb or a noun.

> **1** pollinate (v) **2** pollinator (n)

4.5 Point out to students that they are not necessarily supposed to know the answers to these questions, but that thinking about the answers will help them to gain familiarity with the topic within the text.

> **1** flies, butterflies, beetles, wasps, bumblebees, ants
> **2** 90%
> **3** 9
> **4** several million
> **5** wind
> The excerpt would be relevant, as it includes useful background information on bees and what they do within the context of an ecosystem of flowering plants.

4.6 After having discussed the answers to **4.5** and before reading the text, ask students to read through quickly and find the answers to the questions they could not answer previously. Check students' answers and get feedback from the whole class.

> **Optional extension**
>
> Depending on the level of the class, it may also be useful to explain that having to use the text to answer the questions helped them to try and understand the text in a real-world authentic manner. Advise them that they can use this technique themselves if they have a text to read in another class. All they need to do is look at the title and to create some questions which will cause them to look into the meaning of the text. If they are unsure which questions to ask, direct them towards the common *Wh-* questions such as *what, why, where, who* and *when.*

> **1** yes **2** yes **3** yes **4** yes **5** no

4.7

> **Optional lead-in**
>
> Help students to understand the importance of using guiding questions by doing this activity. Before the beginning of the class, put a pencil on the floor at the back of the classroom. Tell students that you have lost something and ask them to help you find it in the classroom. Don't tell them what it is that you have lost. Start to look around the class as if you are searching for something. Students are likely to start asking what it is that you have lost. Tell them that it doesn't matter and that they should just keep looking. After a few minutes, pretend to remember and tell them that you are looking for a pencil. Hopefully this will speed up the search and one of them will find your pencil at the back of the class. When the pencil has been found, ask students to sit down again and to think about the process they just undertook. The point to make is that it is difficult to find things when you don't know what you're looking for, but if you can focus on a particular thing, then the activity becomes easier and more targeted.

Encourage students to go through the text and underline or highlight the sections which answer Katya's questions from **4.5**.

The text has information that answers all of Katya's questions, with the exception of question 5. Ask students to consider what the role of human beings might be in the pollination process. They should be able to suggest artificial pollination as part of conservation. Refer the class to articles on the importance of pollination and bees to human food sources.

> **1** It was a good way to focus her reading and ensure that she was looking for information that is relevant to her essay.
> **2** Students should understand more.
> **3** yes
> **4** reading and note-taking

Optional extension

If there is sufficient time, ask the class to read some of the facts on these websites, which relate to bees and ecology, for further information:

http://www.canadatop.com/article/Bees
http://entomologyfreaks.tribe.net/thread/e33ecfa7-5319-47ca-a9ba-126b15ed5243
ftp://ftp.fao.org/docrep/fao/012/i0842e/i0842e04.pdf
http://www.centerforabetterlife.com/eng/magazine/article_detail.lasso?id=178
http://www.hobos.de

Note

See the Grammar and vocabulary section for extension and further practice.

5 Grammar in context: noun phrases

5.1 Sentence 2 is from the original text. The information is given in a more economic way and is more typical of written language.
Sentence 1 spreads the information across more clauses and is more typical of spoken language.

Write one or two similar sentences on the board which are more informal and used for speaking. Ask students to rewrite them more concisely using fewer words.

5.2 For questions 1 and 2, encourage students to look for more than one word, as noun and verb phrases consist of more than one word.

1 noun phrases: 1, 4
verb phrases: 2, 3, 5
2 more verbs
3 longer noun phrases

5.3
a a 3   b 4   c 1   d 2
b a 3   b 4   c 1   d 2

Writing

6 Paragraph building

6.1 Remind students about the importance of moving from general to specific in paragraph structure. This should help them to work out the answer.

a Description 2

6.2 Explain to students that this activity is working backwards to show how a plan was constructed to write a paragraph which follows the 'general to specific' approach. Students often find it difficult to plan, and the tendency is to jump in too quickly. Make

it clear that investing time at this stage can really help to get the paragraph and essay structure right.

a Main idea: bees **most important pollinators of flowering plants**
Supporting ideas: other pollinators, e.g. **butterflies, beetles, etc.**
80% plants **pollinated by insects**
85% **insect-pollinated plants – by bees**
90% fruit trees **pollinated by bees**
170,000 flowering plant species **pollinated by bees**
40,000 flowering plants **dependent on bees**
9 species **of honeybees pollinate about 40,000 plants**
b 2

6.3 Students discuss in pairs what they think a topic sentence is and what its function is. Not all students will know this technical term, but at least one or two should be able to describe that a topic sentence is a sentence at the start of a paragraph indicating the general matter to be discussed later in that paragraph.

a Sentence 2 is preferable. It is general enough to introduce the topic of the paragraph.
Sentence 1 is too general and doesn't include the key piece of information about bees visiting the flowers in one day.
b No, it doesn't. Not all paragraphs have concluding sentences.

6.4 Explain to students that writing a paragraph, like the larger task of writing an essay, follows a formula through which a point is made and an argument is described. It is a delicate balance which starts with introducing an idea, then supporting and elaborating upon it.

2 ✗ – They should not be too general; there needs to be a focus.
3 ✓
4 ✓
5 ✗ – The supporting ideas should all relate to the topic of the paragraph as a whole, and new information should not be introduced.
6 ✓

6.5 Before students start their gist read, ask them to apply the skills they have developed so far in predicting the content by looking at the first few lines of the text. To encourage gist reading, give students just five minutes to read and glean an initial understanding of the text.

1 b   2 b

6.6   **1** pesticide(s)   **2** crop(s)

6.7 👥 Students start at the beginning and work progressively through the text. As indicated, they should underline the main idea in each paragraph. When they identify the paragraph with the missing 'main idea', they should work with their partner to write this sentence. Collect the different example sentences from the pairs and write them on the board. The class can vote to decide which sentence works the best.

> **a** Paragraph 1: The absence of honeybees from an ecosystem can have an extremely negative impact on human beings.
> Paragraph 2: Problems with honeybee populations are occurring all around the world.
> Paragraph 3: ✗
> Paragraph 4: The change from small family farms to large industrial farms has had a negative effect on the natural environments of bees.
> **b** Suggested answer: The loss of bees is as big an environmental problem as global warming.

6.8

> **Optional lead-in**
>
> As an introduction to this activity, students brainstorm possible solutions to the bee problem. Write a list of the suggested solutions on the board and try to evaluate, as a class, which solution might be the most viable.

👤 / 👥 Where possible, students complete this activity as individual work, but if there are weaker students in the group, allow them to work together to write the paragraph. When they have finished, students review each others' work. Ask one or two students to read their paragraphs to the rest of the class and, if there is time, make copies of the paragraphs so that students can see a wide range of different suggestions.

> See the model answer on page 26.

7   Grammar in context: present perfect

7.1 Explain to students that we use the present perfect to talk about a less specific point in the past, but when we become more specific, we use the past simple. We also usually use the present perfect when we need to describe something that took place in the past, but is relevant now. Sometimes we use words like *already / just / not ... yet* with the present perfect.

I feel really full. I've just finished my dinner.

I haven't eaten dessert yet, but I've already eaten my main course.

> **a** **1** b   **2** b   **3** b   **4** b
> **b** **1** 1, 4
>   **2** 2, 3
> **c** **1** have
>   **2** has
>   **3** focused
> **d** **1** Sentence b) is correct.
>   **2** Sentence b) uses the past simple. Sentence a) uses the present perfect.
>   **3** It is not possible to use the present perfect together with specific points of time in the past.

7.2

> **a** 1
> **b** yes (This was focused on in Unit 1.)
> **c** **a** show, find, indicate, suggest, argue, find
>   **b** They all include a name (or names) and a date.
>   **c** In the academic examples, it is possible to use the present perfect with an exact date (the date of publication of the book or article being cited).

7.3

> **2** have indicate**d**
> **3** **has** pointed out
> **4** **have** concluded
> **5** have point**ed** out
> **6** **has** indicated
> **7** has show**n**
> **8** **have** argued

7.4

> **2** have asked
> **3** has indicated
> **4** has killed
> **5** was
> **6** showed

Grammar and vocabulary

- Word families
- Quantifying expressions
- Noun phrases
- Clause structure
- Present perfect and past simple

1 Word families

Optional lead-in

In order to focus students on the two verbs *analyse* and *identify*, divide the class into two teams and allocate each team one of the verbs. Ask them to write as many sentences as they can using the verb they have been allocated.

Before moving ahead with the exercises associated with word forms, make sure students understand the differences between verbs, nouns and adjectives.

1.1 **1** identify **2** analyse **3** identify

1.2a

Verb	Nouns	Adjectives
analyse	**1 analysis** (thing)	**1** analytic
	2 analyst (person)	**2 analytical**
identify	**1 identification**	**1** identifying
	2 identity	**2 identifiable**

1.2b
1 analyst
2 analysis
3 analytic
4 analytical

1.3
2 analysis
3 analytical
4 identification
5 analyse

2 Quantifying expressions

Optional lead-in

There are lots of useful websites which give further explanations on how to use numbers in English. Look at the following site for further guidance: http://www.grammarbook.com/numbers/numbers.asp.

2.1 They are all followed by numbers or percentages.

2.2 **a 1** b **2** d **3** a **4** c
b approximately

2.3
1 in all, in total, as many as, up to, is estimated to be about, is thought to be about
2 several, many
3 several

2.4 Suggested answers
1 **In all**, 90% of plants on Earth are angiosperms, also known as 'flowering plants'.
2 **In total**, the number of species of flowering plants are more than 230,000.
3 The three largest flowering plant families are sunflowers, orchids and legumes (peas), which include **as many as** 62,000 species.
4 The number of plants in the orchid family is **thought to be** 24,000 different species.
5 **Up to** 40% of flowering plants in California in the US belong to **several** key plant families.
6 The number of species of seagrasses (marine angiosperms) is **estimated to be about** 50.
7 **Quite a few** species of seagrasses are found along the Pacific Coast of the US.

Optional extension

Test students' knowledge of how to read and speak the numbers that they see in sentences. Write a series of numbers, percentages, fractions, dates and decimal figures on the board and ask students to make and read sentences out loud.

3 Noun phrases

3.1

	Articles, possessives, etc. (determiners)	Adjectives, adverbs, nouns (pre-modifiers)	Head noun	Prepositional phrase (complement)
1	few		flowers	
2	a	single insect	species	
3	the		list	of flowering plants
4		most	flowering plants	
5	a	single	colony	of honeybees
6	the	high	amount	of flowers

3.2
1 all flower <u>types</u>
2 most <u>regions</u> of the world
3 the <u>number</u> of flowering plant species
4 the enormous <u>adaptability</u> of single bees
5 these reliable pollen <u>transporters</u>

4 Clause structure

4.1 phrases

4.2
1 noun
2 verb
3 noun
4 preposition

4.3
1 noun phrase
2 verb phrase
3 noun phrase
4 prepositional phrase

4.4 **a** 2 **b** 1 **c** 3 **d** 4

4.5
1 The bees (*subject* (noun phrase))
inform (*verb phrase*)
one another (*object* (noun phrase))
about newly discovered areas of flowers.
(*prepositional phrase*)
2 Flowering plants (*subject* (noun phrase))
have done (*verb phrase*)
their best (*object* (noun phrase))
to make themselves interesting for honeybees.
(*prepositional phrase*)

5 Present perfect and past simple

5.1
2 have become
3 have been
4 began
5 cost
6 have improved

Model answer

6.8 Model answer

One current solution to the bee pollination problem is moving bee populations around a country. For example, in Australia in the past few years, beekeepers have moved hives to different locations up to six times. This means bees have been able to pollinate different crops at different times of the year. As many as 500 beehives can be moved at a time. Brown (2010) has pointed out that this idea could be an answer for the future of bee pollination.

Lecture skills A

```
PREPARING FOR LECTURES
· Talking about products
· Vocabulary for the context
LISTENING
· Listening for gist and detail
LANGUAGE FOCUS
· If structures 1
· Vocabulary: key expressions
· Pronunciation: emphasising words
FOLLOW-UP
· Organising notes
· Further listening
```

Preparing for lectures

1 Talking about products

Explain to students that thinking about a topic and, if possible, discussing it can help both in the research process and for simply getting your mind in tune. This exercise, which focuses on preparing for lectures, assists in guiding students around a topic using their existing knowledge.

1.1 Suggest that students think of something they buy frequently or something they own and like.

If necessary, you can allocate different groups different kinds of product, such as computer goods or DIY equipment. If some students finish quickly, extra questions could be supplied, e.g.

Is it something disposable or built to last?

What's the main/unique selling point of the product?

How is it marketed?

1.2 👥 While students are explaining their products, go around the classroom and check that they are on task and communicating effectively.

1.3 While students are listing their products, encourage them to think of the reason why they have chosen that particular ranking, as well as compiling the list. Different approaches with different groups may be a useful source for discussion or debate.

2 Vocabulary for the context

2.1 Using a dictionary will help students who may be struggling with this activity, and it will also help to develop skills in identifying useful definitions. If there is a weaker group member, you could make them the group leader and allow them to check answers using the dictionary.

> **a** *Products* and *goods* are things that are made to be bought and sold; a *commodity* can be both products (or goods) or natural resources that can be bought, sold or traded.
> **b** All except 3 are services.

2.2 If necessary, remind students what *collocation* is by reference to earlier units in the Student's Book. Encourage them to try and fill in the gaps before they use their dictionaries.

> **1** fiscal   **2** revenue   **3** scarcity   **4** state

2.3
> **Optional lead-in**
>
> This activity looks at word families and word forms. Before you begin, help students to revise their understanding of word forms by writing *verb*, *noun*, *adjective* and *adverb* on the board and asking students to give you some examples from word families that they are familiar with. Again, looking back at earlier units in the Student's Book will provide a range of examples.

> **a a** All are nouns.
> **b 1** consumption
>   **2** consumer(s)
>   **3** consumerism
> **c** consumerism

Listening

3 Listening for gist and detail

3.1 🔊 A.1

> **1** He gives definitions of key economic terms.
> **2** c
> **3** In general, he has good eye contact with his audience and he is not overly dependent on his notes.
> **4** Yes, he uses it to emphasise key terms mentioned in the lecture.

3.2
1 whom; how
2 goods; public
3 price; shoes
4 public; governments; consume; national
5 public; pay
6 whom; society
7 how; different; problem

3.3
| 2 F | 3 NG | 4 T | 5 NG |
6 F 7 T

Language focus

4 *If* structures 1

4.1 (A.2) Before you watch, prepare students for the focus on *if* structures by creating an example passage yourself similar to the one in the lecture. Ask students to suggest why they think *if* structures are used in this way. If students are familiar with the terminology, ask them to identify which tense is often used with *if* (the conditional).

1 is   2 go   3 want   4 have   5 are
6 won't

4.2 If you mentioned the conditional tense in **4.1**, ask students to explain why they think this tense is used. This may help prepare for the questions that follow.

1 real and possible
2 Example 1: if the consumer is not willing …
3 Examples 2 & 3: if you go downtown …, If you are not willing …

5 Vocabulary: key expressions

5.1 Ensure that students understand that they have to choose the best option for each sentence.

1 a   2 b   3 b   4 c   5 b

5.2
1 this
2 talk
3 differences

6 Pronunciation: emphasising words

6.1 (A.3) This section focuses on stress and emphasis in pronunciation. In order to introduce students to the concept, before you watch the lecture, give students an instruction without putting any emphasis on the key elements of the sentence.

This might be something like: *Please remember to study hard this weekend.* Repeat the same sentence immediately afterwards, putting extra emphasis and stress on the words *Please*, *remember*, *hard* and *this*. Ask students to comment on the difference and to explain why one is more effective than the other.

1 He stresses a lot of words.
2 Because it is early in the lecture, it is likely that he wants the audience to understand key words and terms, so he is using stress to focus on them.

6.2
a Stressed syllables underlined
   Econom<u>ics</u>. Econom<u>ics</u> is the <u>study</u> of <u>how</u> society de<u>cides</u> <u>about</u> <u>three</u> <u>key</u> <u>things</u>. <u>What</u> to pro<u>duce</u>. For <u>whom</u> to pro<u>duce</u> and how <u>much</u> to pro<u>duce</u>. <u>What</u> do we mean when we <u>say</u> <u>what</u> to pro<u>duce</u>. We mean <u>what</u> <u>kind</u> of <u>different</u> <u>goods</u> to pro<u>duce</u>. There are broades … <u>broadly</u> <u>speaking</u> two kind … kinds of <u>categories</u> of <u>goods</u>. The <u>private</u> sector goods and <u>public</u> sector goods. <u>Goods</u> that … they are pro<u>duced</u> by <u>private</u> <u>companies</u> and these are called <u>private</u> <u>goods</u> and <u>goods</u> that they are pro<u>duced</u> by <u>governments</u> and these are called <u>public</u> <u>sec</u>tor <u>goods</u>.
b Group 1

Follow-up

7 Organising notes

7.1 To introduce this section, start a discussion where you ask students to discuss their experience of note-taking and the difficulties they have faced. Ask the class which note-taking strategies they find useful and practical, and what they find to be the biggest challenges.

1 produce   2 private   3 governments
4 distribution   5 choices

Optional extension

PHOTOCOPIABLE
Using symbols in note-taking page 113
(instructions page 104)

7.2

Suggested answers
1 Most students find it difficult to make well-organised and structured notes during the lecture. This is because it is hard to concentrate on understanding the information at the same time as writing down key points.
2 It is a good idea to organise notes at home because it is a good way to revise lecture content, and it means students have a neater record of the information in the lecture. Rough notes taken during the lecture can be difficult to understand at a later date.

8 Further listening

(A.4) Go through the two bullet points with students before watching the extract, so that they know what they are listening for. Use the photocopiable slides on page 126 to help if necessary.

Optional extension

As an additional listening activity, ask students to type 'consumerism' into the YouTube search engine and to watch a relevant video while taking notes. This task could be set for homework and discussed in the next class.

3 Indications and trends

<table>
<tr><td>

Unit aims

READING

· Deciding what to read for an essay
· Approaches to note-taking 1
· Grammar in context: past perfect

WRITING

· Planning the main paragraphs of an essay
· Writing a short report
· Vocabulary in context: language for describing trends

LISTENING AND SPEAKING

· Giving advice
· Asking for help

</td></tr>
</table>

Getting started

1 What do you know?

1.1

> **Optional lead-in**
>
> Books closed. As an introduction to this section, tell students that you will be discussing economics in this unit (as they did in Lecture skills A). To focus them on the subject, ask them to consider the current economic situation in their own country and the country where you are teaching them. If they struggle, ask students who are studying business or economics to take the lead.

Ask students to discuss potential sources of information for definitions. Elicit some possible reasons why Wikipedia may not be the most reliable of sources. Students should be able to point out that anyone can go into it and make changes. Make the point that it is reasonable to use it as a way of getting an initial understanding of something, but that it shouldn't be relied upon to be the definitive answer or used as a reference in a formal essay.

> Both words have a similar meaning because they refer to a time when economic activity is not healthy. Some would argue that a depression is more serious than a recession. Recessions tend to be cyclical and are expected, while depressions are more major events that occur less frequently. In the definition of a **depression**, specific reference is made to the loss of jobs, whereas it is not in the definition for **recession**.

1.2 👤 / 👥 Students can make notes on questions 1 to 3 either on their own or in pairs. Ask students to reflect on their own knowledge and experience.

> **Suggested answers**
> 1 Businesses close, people lose jobs, people save money rather than spend it.
> 3 Governments can sometimes help businesses and society by cutting taxes, lowering interest rates and increasing government spending.

1.3 👥 / 👥 Students can compare notes in pairs or groups. Get feedback from the whole class once they have had a chance to compare notes and share information.

Reading

2 Deciding what to read for an essay

2.1 👤 Ask students to do this activity individually first, before comparing their answers with a partner. Check that they have identified the key words that will drive the main areas within this essay title.

> 1 <u>Outline</u> the <u>factors</u> that <u>led to</u> the Great Depression of the 1930s. <u>Analyse</u> what you believe were the <u>main causes</u> of this depression.

2.2 Explain that it is important to narrow your focus when undertaking research so that you identify the correct type of information which is relevant to the particular essay.

> 1, 2, 4

> **Optional extension**
>
> [PHOTOCOPIABLE]
>
> Choosing internet sources page 114 (instructions page 104).

3 Approaches to note-taking 1

3.1 👥 For this exercise, it may be useful to pair students with a partner who has more specific knowledge relating to this topic. In the previous lessons, the topic focus was different from this, so make the point that, as you move through the Student's Book, at different points, each student is likely to find different topics which align with their particular specialism.

> b 5   c 6   d 2   e 8   f 3
> g 1   h 4

3.2 Before showing students the options for this question, give them two minutes to skim the text for a general gist understanding. After the time has elapsed, ask them to give a verbal general description of the topic. Next, show them options 1–4 and invite them to select the correct answer.

> Option 3 is correct. Some learners may feel option 2 is correct because there is some statistical information in the text. However, it is not very detailed. For example, in paragraph 2, the increase in the labour force is given as a percentage, and other information about health and education is not supported by statistical information on infant mortality and school attendance.

3.3 | Information in the text is relevant to the essay title.

Ask students to support the reasons why they think this is the case. This will help them to start to consider how support can be provided from this source.

3.4 The best approach for this activity, if there is time, is to ask students to read each of the paragraphs and to consider what the main point would be without the aid of the options. When they have read, then ask them to look at the options and select the best one.

> **Paragraph 1:** a
> **Paragraph 2:** b
> **Paragraph 3:** b
> **Paragraph 4:** a

Refer students to this table, which lists some common abbreviations that can be used in note-taking:

+ or &	and
–	minus, without
=	equals
≠	not equal to
≈	approximately equal to
<	less than
>	greater than
⬈ or ⇧	rise, increase
⬊ or ⇩	decrease, fall, reduction
⇨ or ∴	therefore, thus
⇨	causes
x	not, wrong
#	number
✱	special, noteworthy
/	per (e.g. £50/day instead of *fifty pounds per day*)

3.5 Encourage students to approach this task systematically. They should tick off each of the bullets that they can find, rather than focusing on what they cannot find.

👥 Give students a time limit and ask them to discuss their observations in pairs before feeding back to the class.

> **a** The incorrect information is: workers liked using new technology. The text indicates that technology was able to exploit natural resources, but there is no mention of workers or entrepreneurs liking new technology.
> **b** missing information: children healthy + education; science & technology

3.6 | **a** Paragraph 1

> **Focus on your subject**
>
> Ask students to write down some abbreviations relevant to their own subject, then compare with a partner.

3.7 | **Optional lead-in**
>
> In preparation for this task, ask students to think about how they remember what they have read in the past. Ask them if they have had previous experience of taking notes on their reading at school or for other purposes. In order to illustrate the importance of note-taking, give students an article which contains a range of statistical information.
>
> 👥👥 Divide the class into two groups. Ask both groups to read the article, but only allow half of the class to take notes. Later, ask both groups to give you specific details without looking at the text. It is likely that the group which has taken notes will be more easily able to answer the questions without looking at the text.

> **1** They help to summarise main ideas in a text.
> **2** main points made in the text that are relevant for your essay; any useful statistical information
> **3** It is likely that students will be tempted to copy the original. Copying from the text is plagiarism.

4 Grammar in context: past perfect

4.1 In this section, the past perfect tense is introduced and students discover some of the rules. Another way of explaining this tense to students is to tell them that we use the past perfect simple tense in order to move further back in time when we are already talking about something in the past. It can help focus on the fact that something had already happened at the time we are discussing. Use the board to draw a time line showing now and two points in the past, one further in the past than the other.

> a 2
> b c
> c 1 repeated events   2 yes   3 single event
>   4 before

4.2
> a subject + **had** + past **participle**
> b 2 single
>   3 events
>   4 before
>   5 then
>   6 choose
>   7 past
>   8 necessary
>   9 past

Writing

5 Planning the main paragraphs of an essay

5.1
> **Optional lead-in**
>
> This section starts with essay planning, so it will be useful to ask students to think about the purpose of essay planning. Ask them how and why essay planning can be useful, and what their experiences of essay planning have been in the past. What sort of information do they think should be included in an essay plan?

Elicit from students the importance of devising and following a plan, so that they can be sure to build into the essay all the required elements and argument, as well as ideas from their reading. Use the analogy of using a map to keep the best route in sight. Also try to get them to go through the different structural elements they can remember, or are already aware of. At least some students will be aware of some of the structural elements of the introduction, main body and conclusion. This is a good point at which to iron out any misconceptions or cultural differences in essay writing.

> 2 f
> 3 e
> 4 a
> 5 d
> 6 b

5.2
> 1 a paragraph
> 2 key points
> 3 No, it's only an outline.
> 4 It helps organise ideas from reading.

5.3 Refer students to the discussion they had in **5.1** as they start this task; this should help them to think of the best ways to refine the essay plan.

Listening and speaking

6 Giving advice

6.1 Before starting this activity, ask students to review the discussions they had relating to the essay plan. What previous experiences have they had with essay planning, and what comments did they make about the essay plan? In which ways did they suggest it could be improved? This reflection and discussion will be good preparation for the listening. Then play recording (◄)3.1).

6.2
> 1 She wrote a similar essay the previous year.
> 2 Two paragraphs are probably not needed for the essay because they are not relevant to the essay question: the one on the financial system and the one on employment.
> 3 fifteen hundred (1,500) words
> 4 to make the essay more relevant
> 5 He's going to think about it.

6.3 (◄)3.2)
> 1 I think you could
> 2 If I were you
> 3 Why don't you think about
> 4 I'd suggest
> 5 I think you should probably

6.4
> 1 c
> 2 She is diplomatic, probably because she realises that Dmitry has done a lot of reading and thinking in preparing the plan, and she doesn't want to show a lack of respect for his effort.
> 3 no

6.5 (◄)3.2) Play extracts 1–5 again.
> a The tone of her voice rises. Gunilla does this to make her advice sound more polite. A flat tone could make her sound aggressive.

6.6
> 1 I think you could
> 2 why don't you think about
> 3 if I were you
> 4 I'd suggest

6.7 Refer students back to the language points introduced in Unit 1, which include some focus on 'asking for help'. This could be particularly relevant to this unit.

7 Asking for help

7.1 Allow students a few minutes to discuss the question in small groups before playing recording ◀)3.3. Students may find it helpful to make brief notes as they listen, which they can then expand into lists of similarities and differences.

Writing

8 Writing a short report

8.1 Explain to students that the article can be used for research purposes and that the report itself is also a form of research for the essay. Try to show students that this kind of activity is useful for understanding a subject more deeply and collecting relevant information. It is also typical of the sort of activity that a student in a UK university is expected to engage in.

8.2 Yes, the article contains useful information.

8.3
1 apprenticeship
2 foothold
3 out of work
4 smooth transition

8.4 Refer students back to the note-taking patterns in section 3 and encourage them to record the key points as briefly and accurately as possible.

9 Vocabulary in context: language for describing trends

9.1 Optional lead-in

As an introduction to this activity, show students a series of graphs such as those below:

A Sales of Product X (million £) 2003–2012

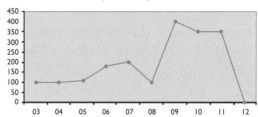

B Prices of shares ($) in Company Y 2003–2010

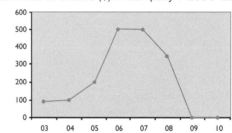

With books closed, students describe the trends they observe in the graphs, and focus on the language required to describe the discernible fluctuations. Ask them to highlight the different types of movement/ changes in the graph by highlighting or circling the places on the graph.

Encourage students to think of the language required, including verbs such as *rise* and *decrease*, as well as adjectives like *dramatic* or *steep*. This should help to prepare them for the questions in the Student's Book and get them thinking in the right context.

a 1 rose
  2 has climbed
b 2 has climbed

9.2
2 decreased
3 dramatically
4 steady
5 increase
6 beginning
7 downward
8 lowest

9.3

1 ↗ rose, increased, climbed ↘ fell, decreased
2 ↗ rise, increase, climb ↘ drop, fall, decrease
3 adverbs: *slightly*, *slowly*, etc.
4 adjectives: *minimal*, *slight*, etc.
5 the start/beginning of a(n) upward/downward trend
6 It reached the highest/lowest point.
7 past simple
8 present simple or present continuous
9 present perfect simple or continuous

9.4

1 b
2 c
3 a

9.5

1 sharp / sudden / dramatic
2 rise / increase / climb
3 in
4 highest
5 point
6 decreased / fell
7 steadily / gradually
8 rose / increased / climbed
9 suddenly / sharply / dramatically
10 a
11 sudden / sharp / dramatic
12 decrease / fall / drop

9.6 If students struggle to find appropriate data, give them this table.

UK unemployment rates (%): by gender and age, 1991 to 1999
Social Trends 30

	1991	1992	1993	1994	1995	1996	1997	1998	1999
Males: 16–17	15.4	17.7	18.5	18.8	18.9	21.2	19.3	18.0	21.6
Males: 18–24	15.7	19.0	21.1	19.2	17.7	17.1	14.8	13.0	12.5

source: Labour Force Survey, Office for National Statistics 2000

See the model answer on page 37.

Grammar and vocabulary

- Corpus language
- Past simple
- Past perfect
- Language to describe statistics
- Words for economic graphs

1 Corpus language

Optional lead-in

Give students copies of the grid below (but with no bold letters) and ask them to find the topic-related vocabulary. If they need help, you can give them the list of words (see below). This activity can be extended by making similar puzzles of your own to give students extra practice. Go to puzzlemaker.com, where you can create the same sort of activities for free, using different vocabulary.

D	E	J	U	Y	S	M	D	E	X	L	W	D	Q	Y
A	E	X	K	L	I	H	O	N	A	K	E	L	C	X
K	L	F	F	M	M	B	L	T	X	V	A	I	S	Z
D	H	I	L	C	Q	O	I	R	A	T	L	C	Q	V
J	D	N	X	A	A	P	Q	E	Y	A	T	B	V	U
F	N	F	P	P	T	T	Q	P	O	W	H	V	K	R
O	Z	L	O	I	O	I	F	R	T	J	D	N	J	C
Q	O	A	X	T	G	F	O	E	O	U	T	P	U	T
X	I	T	X	A	B	G	E	N	D	K	P	R	T	K
Q	N	I	R	L	R	G	I	E	C	I	O	H	I	I
T	L	O	X	P	M	Z	G	U	X	O	Q	M	L	R
K	E	N	L	S	R	S	M	R	E	U	M	K	S	H
S	T	O	C	K	M	A	R	K	E	T	J	E	B	V
X	W	Q	C	N	X	E	V	Q	Z	Z	R	L	P	H
I	N	C	O	M	E	K	L	M	D	X	X	V	D	B

deflation
entrepreneur
wealth
inflation
capital
output
stock market
income

1.1 indicate (v), indication (n)

1.2
1 clearly
2 findings; data
3 give
4 general; clear

2 Past simple

2.1
a a ✓   b ✗   c ✗   d ✓
b **1** *be* (I) **2** *have* (I) **3** *come* (I) **4** *believe* (R)

2.2 Refer students back to the guidance provided earlier in the unit, in both the Student's Book and this book, with regard to the past simple. Remind students before they begin that it is a negative instance of the past simple that they are looking for. The negative should help them to identify the verb in the text if they are unsure.

Employment and output <u>did not fully improve</u> …

2.3
1 -ed
2 not
3 base

2.4
2 got
3 continued
4 made
5 was

3 Past perfect

3.1 👥 / 👥👥 Tell each pair or group of students that they have to reach a consensus agreement on which of the sentences includes the past perfect before moving on to the next. Refer them back to the explanations and exercises on the past perfect earlier in this unit if any further guidance is needed.

1 past perfect
2 past simple form of *have*
3 past perfect
4 past perfect
5 past simple form of *have*
6 past simple form of semi-modal *have to*
7 past perfect
8 past participle of *have* – part of present perfect form
9 past perfect
10 past participle form of semi-modal *have to* – part of present perfect form

3.2 👥 For this activity, ask pairs to answer questions 1 and 2, and to discuss their answers before getting ready to feed back to the rest of the class. Choose a group that you think has grasped the concept, and ask them to explain the rules which have led them to their decisions.

a In example 1, the past perfect is used in the second part of the sentence (*had forgotten*, *had been*), whereas in example 2 the simple past is used (*forgot*, *was*). They are both correct.
b The emphasis occurs in example 1, where the past perfect is used.
c In example 2, the prepositional phrase *in 1973* helps us to understand the sequence of events. This signals that the crisis occurred prior to 2008.

3.3
1 past simple only
2 past perfect possible
3 past perfect possible
4 past simple only
5 past perfect possible
6 past simple only
7 past simple only
8 past simple only
9 past perfect possible
10 past perfect possible

4 Language to describe statistics

4.1 Refer students back to the table earlier in the unit for examples of vocabulary to use. It may also be useful to draw on any resources that you have which relate to IELTS Writing Task 1, which usually requires the description of a chart or diagram using this same sort of vocabulary.

1 climbed
2 fell
3 dramatically
4 gradually
5 slight

4.2 Suggested answers
1 fall
2 steady
3 downward
4 suddenly

5 Words for economic graphs

5.1 It will be useful to start this activity using a dictionary to make sure that students understand each of the vocabulary items. You could also ask students to use a thesaurus to compile a list of synonyms or antonyms.

1 invaluable
2 simultaneously
3 interpretation
4 apparent

OECD* Unemployment Rates – Percentage of labour force

	2007	2008	2009
OECD total	5.7	6.1	8.6
Major seven**	5.4	5.9	8.4
European area	7.5	7.6	9.2
European Union	7.1	7.0	9.2
The US	4.6	5.8	9.8

* Organisation for Economic Co-operation and Development

** Major seven industrialised countries: Canada, France, Germany, Italy, Japan, the UK, the USA

Data taken from OECD news release: OECD Harmonised Unemployment Rates 9 November 2009. http://www.oecd.org/dataoecd/1/38/44038826.pdf

9.6 Model answer

The table shows the unemployment rate of young males in the UK between 1991 and 1999. The males are divided into two age groups: those who are 16 and 17 years old and those who are aged between 18 and 24. There is a gradual increase in unemployment rates for the 16- and 17-year-olds from 1991 until 1999, when unemployment for that age group reached its highest point of 21.6%. In 1996, the rate was also high, at 21.2%, but it dropped slowly over the next two years before rising again in 1999. In the second age group, unemployment rose steadily for the first three years of the decade, then dropped from 1994 onwards, to reach its lowest point of 12.5% in 1999. This is in sharp contrast to the unemployment rate of 16- and 17-year-olds. Between 1996 and 1997, there was a sharp drop of 2.3% in unemployment rates for 18- to 24-year-olds. This was the biggest decrease of the decade.

4 The information age

Unit aims

READING
- Interactive reading
- Grammar in context: phrases of frequency
- Reading for the main ideas in a text
- Grammar in context: prepositional phrases

LISTENING AND SPEAKING
- Outlining issues and putting forward your point of view

WRITING
- Drafting and building arguments

Optional extension

If your college is based on a campus or has a communal foyer area, you could ask students to conduct the survey during class time. Make sure you prepare students for the dangers of approaching strangers, and prepare them for the fact that some people they approach may refuse to respond or ignore them. If there is sufficient time, students could conduct the survey with friends or family, or even create an electronic version of the survey which can be distributed and collected free of charge via a website such as www.surveymonkey.com.

Getting started

1 A survey: the information age

1.1 To introduce this topic, start by asking students to list all the sources that they commonly get information from. Given developments in information technology over the last 20–30 years, the Internet is likely to be the number-one suggestion, although the responses may be ranked differently according to the context of your teaching, the resources available and the age range in your class. Once students have listed some options, such as the Internet, television, books, newspapers, etc., ask them to consider the benefits and disadvantages of each source.

> social and ethical issues, use of computers, information age

1.2 👥 Books open. Divide the questions amongst the groups. You may need to modify some of your questions based on the students you are working with, and the likely access that they have to ICT. For example, if students are unlikely to have access to online shopping due to socio-economic or cultural differences, then omit or revise this question.

1.3, 1.4 Encourage groups to select questions which they feel will be most pertinent to the people they are able to use the survey with. Exchange sets of questions between groups to help identify any errors or leading questions. For example, avoid any questions which steer respondents in a particular way: a question such as 'All intelligent people use the Internet regularly; how often do you use the Internet?' risks pushing the respondent to give a particular response.

1.5 Discuss the results with the rest of the class. Encourage students to take notes on the question areas that were explored by the other groups. In this way, groups can learn from each other, as they focused on different aspects of the information question.

Reading

2 Interactive reading

2.1 This text should not now feel too unfamiliar if students have had time to complete and discuss the previous activities.

2.2
> **b** **1** head noun = technologies
> adjective = cutting-edge
> **2** plural
> **3** examples of more recent technology
> **c** Definition 2

Language note

A noun phrase (NP) has a noun in what is called the 'head position'. The 'pre-head string', if there is one, usually comprises adjectives and determiners.

[NP *the computers*]

[NP *modern computers*]

[NP *the modern computers*]

The head of an NP does not have to be a common or a proper noun. Pronouns can also act as the head of an NP:

[NP I] *read journals*.

The librarian gave [NP *me*] *the wrong book*.

[NP *This*] *is my laptop*.

If the head takes the form of a pronoun, then the NP will usually be comprised solely of the head. This is due to the fact that you can't use determiners or adjectives with pronouns, so there can't be a pre-head element. However, with some pronouns, there may be a post-head part:

[NP *Those who arrive at the lecture late*] *will not be permitted to enter*.

Likewise, numbers or numerals, as they are a sub-class of nouns, can appear as the head of an NP:

[NP *Two of my references*] *were taken from Wikipedia*.

[NP *The first entry in my bibliography*] *is Anderson, 2009*.

2.3 In order to check that students have actually understood these noun phrases, ask them to give examples which illustrate the meanings. For example, a *high-tech surveillance device* could be a GPS Tracker. A *law enforcement official* could be a policeman.

2.4a **Optional lead-in**

Start to introduce the complexities of distinguishing fact from opinion by asking students to complete this quiz. Answers are given in brackets.

1 The Internet is better than a library. (O)	F/O
2 Macs are better than PCs. (O)	F/O
3 Some people enjoy internet browsing. (F)	F/O
4 The UK has the best education system in the world. (O)	F/O
5 Books are more reliable than websites. (O)	F/O
6 YouTube is the best place to watch videos. (O)	F/O
7 You can believe everything you see on BBC TV. (O)	F/O
8 The Internet offers an unlimited source of information. (F)	F/O

There are likely to be some strong opinions, but make it clear that only 3 and 8 have any factual basis.

Explain that even though you might believe something to be true, unless it is based on clearly identifiable

fact, then it has to be considered to be an opinion and is therefore open to discussion or challenge. Tell students that they should start to think like this when they read, and begin to challenge some of the statements, which may actually be based on opinion, although an author may have presented them as a fact.

Explain, with reference to the student's reactions to the first two paragraphs of the text, that her comments on the text show that she is challenging and reading critically.

To do something similar, ask students to think of challenges or counter-arguments to some of the ideas in the fact-or-opinion quiz in the Optional lead-in.

> She agrees with the first point, but questions the second.

2.4b This exercise should be assisted by the preparatory work you have done on critical thinking. This will help students to start thinking of alternative viewpoints and to create possible advantages in response to the disadvantages.

Optional extension

👥 If you feel that students need further preparation, ask pairs to take it in turns to play a game called 'Every cloud has a silver lining'.

One person starts by suggesting a negative situation, for example 'The weather is terrible today', and the other person has to think of how this situation could actually be considered an advantage, for example 'The rain will be good for the plants'.

2.5 For the seminar discussion, it may be useful to choose the group members carefully, so that there is a spread of shy and confident students in each group. You could also allocate different members a particular role, such as chairperson, to help guide the discussion. If there are likely to be a number of discussion areas, set a time limit for each area of discussion.

3 Grammar in context: phrases of frequency

3.1a As an introduction to this activity, give students the list of expressions below and ask them to put them in a table which shows the rank of frequency.

· never	· hardly ever · rarely	· occasionally · once in a while · every now and again · every so often · every two years	
· often · frequently	· quite often	· very often	· always

a 1 b   **2** a

3.1b *Once every two years* is different because it shows definite frequency, as opposed to the other phrases, which show indefinite frequency.

3.1c 👥 Ask students to work in pairs for this activity and to agree on the correct answer before moving on to the next question.

Example 2 sounds unnatural.

3.1d **1** mid
2 front; end

3.2 Refer students back to the rule introduced in the previous exercise. If necessary, show them this table as additional guidance.

Subject	Frequency adverb (mid-position)	Main verb	Object, place or time
I	often	go swimming	in the evenings.
He	always	plays	tennis.
We	usually	go	to the library on Monday afternoons.

Frequency phrase (front position)	Subject	Main verb	Object, place or time	Frequency phrase (end position)
Every now and then	I	go swimming	in the evenings	every now and then.
Every once in a while	He	plays	tennis	every once in a while.
Every Monday afternoon	We	go	to the library	every Monday afternoon.

1 Every now and then, a massive power blackout causes a state of emergency in a major city. (*end position also possible*)
2 Businesses frequently suffer from database crashes that show the need to back up information.
3 Every once in a while, a new and innovative IT product is released on the market. (*end position also possible*)
4 Every so often, an internet virus creates IT chaos around the world. (*end position also possible*)
5 Law enforcement officers occasionally manage to catch computer criminals.

4 Reading for the main ideas in a text

4.1 Ask students to think of how they book their own travel arrangements and what they have noticed about the use of IT to advertise travel and hospitality. Ask them about their experiences of hotel and airline websites. If you have access to the Web, it might be useful to visit the website for an airline such as BA or easyJet. You could also look at the website for a hotel chain such as Holiday Inn or Ibis.

4.2 It gives an overview.

4.3 Don't allow students to use a dictionary at the start of this exercise. Tell them that the whole point is to try and work out the answers through the context. Explain that if this is possible, it is quicker than using a dictionary. You should also point out that this method is what we use in the real world most of the time, as there simply isn't time to use a dictionary.

a 2 brokers
3 option
4 get rid of
5 specials
6 access
7 enhance

b 1 enhance
2 access
3 excess capacity
4 special
5 option
6 get rid of
7 broker

4.4 👤 Ask students to work through the text themselves first to draw up their own list of key points.
👥 / 👥 Once this is done, ask them to work in pairs or threes to compare their list to the one in this exercise. This will also prepare them well for the ordering process.

2 e   **3** h   **4** a   **5** g   **6** b   **7** f   **8** d

4.5 **2** a   **3** f   **4** b   **5** g   **6** e   **7** h   **8** d

4.6

a therefore

b as a result (line 18); so (line 22); thus (line 32); consequently (line 33)

c *As a result thus* and *consequently* normally come at the beginning of a sentence and are followed by a comma.

d Suggested answers

The Internet means tourism companies can make direct sales to customers. **As a result,** there is an increase in customer self-service. Internet customers can make many choices in their own time, **so** sales representatives do not need to spend time with customers while they make decisions about their travel.

Internet customers can buy online where and when they want to, **therefore** there is greater customer satisfaction.

Airlines can sell extra seats cheaply. **Thus,** customers who want a bargain can choose a cheaper flight when the airline needs customers. The Internet allows tourism operators to provide prospective customers with a lot of information, including visual information. **Consequently,** customers can get a lot of specific information about a tourist destination.

5 Grammar in context: prepositional phrases

5.1 Introduce students to prepositional phrases with the following explanation:

A prepositional phrase will start with a **preposition** and finish with a **noun**, noun phrase or gerund (-*ing*), as the 'object' of that preposition.

A prepositional phrase will act in a similar way to an **adjective** or **adverb**.

As an adjective, the prepositional phrase can help to provide the answer to the question: *Which one?*

The book **on my desk** *is borrowed from the University library.*

Which book? **The one on my desk!**

As an adverb, a prepositional phrase can answer questions such as *When?, How?* or *Where?*.

Cheng-Cheng is tired **from yesterday's maths test**.

How did Cheng-Cheng get tired? **From yesterday's maths test.**

> **1** nouns
> **2** a noun phrase
> **3** -*ing*
> **4** yes
> **5** adverb (It adds meaning to the prepositional phrase.)

5.2 Explain to students that they should start by looking at the list of prepositions and then move on to consider each gap by looking at the words which come before and after the missing word. They can also refer to other examples they know of how to use each preposition to guess where they fit if they are still unsure.

This would also make a good dictionary practice activity if students need more help. For example, if students look up the word *rid*, they will find *get rid of* in the rules of usage.

> **2** for
> **3** over
> **4** with
> **5** of
> **6** from

> **Optional extension**
>
> PHOTOCOPIABLE
>
> Understanding prepositional phrases page 115 (instructions page 105)

Listening and speaking

6 Outlining issues and putting forward your point of view

6.1 ◄)4.1 Before students start to listen, ask them to review what they have discussed so far on this subject.

👥 Ask pairs to suggest what the discussion is likely to concentrate on, to focus students on the type of conversation before they start listening.

As a final preparatory question, ask one or two students to explain their personal views on the role played by IT in tourism.

> **1** b
> **2** No. Susanna thinks it is useful, Dan has some doubts, and Pawel has a balanced view.

6.2 ◄)4.1

> **1** booking a flight online and finding it inefficient
> **2** about his aunt, whose personal details were given away to other companies

6.3 This question is based on the unreliability of personal experiences for reference in academic writing. To illustrate this point, ask students to suggest which source of information might be more suitable:

a a journal article based on research, or

b a personal account from an individual person.

Try to show students that **a** is an example of something more reliable, as it is usually based on more thorough and reliable research which has been approved by a publisher.

> No, a personal example of this nature is not appropriate for an essay.

6.4 | They are quite direct.

6.5 (◄)4.2)

> **a** no
> **b** Susanna: *the way I see it is ...; another good point is ...*
> Pawel: *but I sometimes wonder if ...*
> Dan: *I'm beginning to think that ...; let's look at another issue ...*
> Dan: *I have to say ...*
> **c** to introduce the point they are making; to signal to the others that they are about to make a point; to slightly soften the directness of their opinion

6.6 | **2** is
> **3** if
> **4** that (It can be left out.)
> **5** issue
> **6** that (It can be left out.)

6.7 (◄)4.3) 👥 Ask students to work in pairs for this exercise and go around the class listening to check the appropriate usage of stress. Explain to students that *prominent* has the same meaning here as *stressed*.

> **a 2** point **3 some**times **4** be**gin**ning
> **5** an**o**ther **6** say

6.8 Ask students to think about all the ideas they have collected in their discussions and listening about IT and travel/hospitality.

👥 If possible, allocate each of the phrases in section 3 to a group in the class and then go through their ideas as a class to check them.

Writing

7 Drafting and building arguments

7.1 👥 Ask students to work in pairs and to be prepared to describe the features they see in the type of writing which Pawel has completed, as well as answering the questions. Students should be able to say that the writing is in note form, rather than an essay draft or a final essay. Make sure they are able to explain how they can tell that this is in note form.

> **a** notes: He is not writing complete sentences. He is also using abbreviations (*vs., e.g.*) and shortened forms of punctuation: – ; &
> **b** Pawel should now write a first draft using the notes.

7.2 👤 / 👥 Ask students to work on the ordering activity, either in pairs or individually, then select an individual or a pair to feed back to the rest of the class. To help students understand the different stages of a paragraph, you could also draw a flowchart on the board which indicates where each of the different steps fits in.

> **a a** 3 **b** 5 **c** 1 **d** 4 **e** 2
> **b** state, note

7.3 To prepare students for this activity, ask them to explain the aim of research and background reading. Try and get students to explain that research and background reading can provide support for the ideas which are introduced. It should follow naturally that you can ask them how this support can be integrated into writing. This should lead the discussion on to referencing. This will prepare students to be able to identify what is missing from the text in this exercise.

> There are no references to other works used to support the claims made, so there is no evidence of Pawel having done any background reading.

7.4 | **1** notes 1 and 3
> **2** notes 2 and 3 (While note 2 doesn't make explicit mention of information overload, the idea of electronic middle men suggests that customers don't know where to begin looking because there's so much information that can be accessed.)

7.5 Explain to students that it is normal that a first draft should include lots of areas for improvement. When putting together the first draft of an essay, students should try bringing together as many ideas as they can. It is not important at the first-draft stage to focus on details such as spelling or punctuation; it is the ideas that are important. There will be time later to add and remove elements, as well as to improve on structure. Also, for future reference, tell students not to worry about the introduction when writing a first draft. It will only delay the writing process, as they probably won't know what to include if they haven't got a clear idea of how the essay will develop.

> **1** c **2** b **3** d **4** a

7.6 | See the model answer on page 45.

Grammar and vocabulary

- Word building
- Noun phrases
- Phrases of frequency
- Vocabulary families
- Prepositional phrases
- Reporting verbs

1 Word building

1.1

Optional extension

For a range of additional exercises on affixes, show students what is available on http://www.esl-galaxy.com/prefixsuffix.html. This could also be used for homework purposes.

The following tables of prefixes and suffixes could also provide useful guidance if you need to explain the function of different prefixes and suffixes.

Prefix	Meaning
ante-	before
anti-	against/opposite
auto-	self
bi-	two
circum-	around
dis-	not
hyper-	over
hypo-	under
il-	not
im-	not
in-	not; into
inter-	between
ir-	not
mis-	wrong
neo-	new
omni-	all
ploy-	many
post-	after
pre-	before
pro-	for/forward
re-	again
retro-	backward
semi-	half
sub-	below
super-	above
trans-	across
tri-	three
un-	not

Suffix	Meaning
-able, -ible	can be done
-al, -ial	having personal traits of
-ed	past tense
-en	made of
-er	comparative
-est	superlative
-ful	full of
-ic	having characteristics of
-ing	verb form present participle
-ion, -tion, -ation, -ition	act, process
-ity, -ty	state of
-ive, -ative, -itive	adjective form of a noun
-less	without
-ly	characteristic of
-ment	action/process
-ness	state of / condition of
-ous, -eous, -ious	having the qualities of
-s, -es	more than one
-y	characterised by

a 1 un- 2 de- 3 -ation, -ent
  4 -ize, -ed 5 -ed
b impossible = not
  illogical = not
  disagree = opposite action
  non-existent = not
  incorrect = not
  irregular = not
c illegal unclear distrust impatient
  irrational inaccurate

Optional extension

If students need further practice, use the affix tables above to create some additional activities where students have to add affixes to change meaning.

2 Noun phrases

2.1
a problem associated with information

2.2
a explosion
b hardware
c man
d human beings
e divide
f 'have-nots'
g nations

2.4

1 c
2 f
3 a
4 b
5 g
6 d
7 e

Note

There are lots of practice and development activities available online, and a useful one for prepositional phrases can be found at http://esl.about.com/library/quiz/bl_prepphrase1.htm.

3 Phrases of frequency

3.1

Optional extension

Refer students back to the use of frequency phrases earlier in this unit. Ask them to create some sentences using them, before embarking on this activity. This should bring the form and usage back into focus.

1 Every ~~once~~ **so** often
2 almost ~~ever~~ **never**
3 ~~much~~ **very** often
4 sometimes but not ~~frequent~~ **often**
5 once **a** minute; once **an** hour
6 only every once ~~for~~ **in** a while

Once the correct usage has been determined, as above, ask students to think of alternative phrases that have the same meaning and can be used to replace those above.

4 Vocabulary families

4.1

Noun	Verb	Adjective
access	access	accessible
excess	exceed	excessive
option	opt	optional

4.2

1 access
2 exceed
3 excessive
4 accessible
5 opt

5 Prepositional phrases

5.1

1 The Internet allows customers to give feedback directly **_to_** _the seller_.
2 **_In_** _most countries_, there is a variety **_of_** _internet service providers_.
3 The growth **_of_** _IT_ has been seen as an opportunity **_for_** _new business ventures_.
4 Customers noted that there was limited availability **_of_** _telephone support_.
5 Many large companies are unsure how to get rid **_of_** _unwanted old computers_.

6 Reporting verbs

6.1

Optional extension

For extra work on reporting verbs, ask students to agree on the meaning of the verbs listed below. They can use a dictionary to confirm the detail of the meaning, if necessary. Students should create at least five sentences using five of these verbs:

affirm	assert	demonstrate
allege	claim	maintain
argue	contend	predict

2 explains
3 emphasises
4 notes
5 pinpoints
6 describes
  1 + 4, 2 + 6, 3 + 5

6.2

1 describe
2 note
3 pinpoint

6.3

a explain, describe, state, note
b emphasise, pinpoint

6.4

1 that
2 explains / describes
3 emphasises / pinpoints
4 how
5 notes / states
6 emphasises / pinpoints

7.6 Model answer

Finally, those people who can access the Internet easily often find there is too much information to choose from and understand. Morrison (2002) states that consumers may find it takes too much time or is boring to buy online, and, as a consequence, they may decide not to buy anything. A lot of tourist and hospitality companies, for example hotels and car-rental firms, advertise their tourist products through online brokers such as Expedia, which can create a second problem with information overload. Hudson and Lang (2001) note the problem of brokers preventing customers and sellers from having a direct relationship with each other. A possible result is that the tourism company cannot build a relationship with a customer and develop customer loyalty, which is a powerful form of marketing.

Lecture skills B

Preparing for lectures

1 Women scientists in history

1.1 In preparation for this activity, ask students to think of as many famous women from their country and to be ready to explain why the women were well known.

> **1** Mary Somerville
> **2** Hertha Ayrton
> **3** This fact cannot be added to a file.
> **4** Caroline Herschel

2 Vocabulary for the context

2.1 Introduce this section by helping students to understand the types of word that they are looking for. Start students thinking along the two themes of 'women's rights' and 'what people think' by asking them to think about changes in women's rights over the last century, and asking them to think of words which might be used to describe the way in which people think.

> **a** 3, 6
> **b** 1, 2, 4, 5

2.2
> **b** 1   **c** 4   **d** 2   **e** 6   **f** 3

Listening

3 Listening for gist and detail

3.1 **Optional lead-in**

As a precursor to the listening activity, it would be useful to ask students to tell you what they know about the women's rights movement in their country – or in the UK, if the topic has cultural sensitivities in the students' home culture(s). Encourage students to tell you when they think women first got the vote, and when education first became available to women on the same basis as men.

B.1 Make sure students understand what listening for gist involves and go over any previous work of this nature which has involved getting just the main ideas from a listening or written text. Remind them again that this kind of exercise is similar to skimming in reading.

Background information

It may be useful to provide students with the following background information.

In the lecture, the following institutions are talked about.
- *Girton College* – the first women's university college in England, founded in 1869 at Cambridge University
- *Newnham College* – another women-only college at Cambridge University, founded in 1871
- *the Cavendish Laboratory* – the department of physics at Cambridge University
- *the Royal Society* – an institution interested in scientific research and discussion, founded in 1660 in London

> **1** Hertha Ayrton and Mary Somerville
> **2** history

3.2
> **1** No, it wasn't necessary. (Draw students' attention to the fact that only key details were required.)
> **2** reading for gist (Likewise, the task in **3.1** required students to listen for gist.)
> **3** understand the main ideas – the gist of the lecture

3.3a B.1

> **1** She thinks it helps us understand the present and perhaps improve things in the future.
> **2** **Hertha Ayrton:** 1876: went to Girton College, Cambridge; studied in a laboratory at Girton; got a certificate in mathematics – wasn't allowed to graduate (women weren't then); her book *The Electric Arc* helped solve a problem with street lamps; 1902: proposed for fellowship at the Royal Society but turned down because she was married; first woman to read her own paper at the Royal Society
> **Mary Somerville:** didn't go to university because she couldn't go; 1826: published paper in Royal Society journal *Philosophical Transaction*; never allowed to go into Royal Society, so her husband read her paper
> **3** to examine the way that historians have viewed women's role in science

3.3b 👥 In pairs, students work through each summary, considering whether it covers adequately and fully enough the main points in the text. Explain that it is a fine balance between not too little and not too much.

> Summary 1

Language focus

4 Signposting language in lectures

In previous units, students learned about cohesive devices in essays which provide a more formal signpost and help to introduce and mark the function of different sections of a passage.

Signposting in spoken excerpts can be used in this same way, but it can also be used in order to demonstrate the speaker's intention and aim. Give some examples using *going to*, which is the main focus of the next exercise.

For example:

In this next example, I'm going to illustrate the point by referring to a case study.

B.2

4.1
> **Extract 1:** going to be
> **Extract 2:** going to be; going to be
> **Extract 3:** going to go
> **Extract 4:** is going to be
> **Extract 5:** going to talk

4.2
> **1** what is coming in the lecture
> **2** yes
> **3** one after another

5 Pronunciation

5.1 B.3 Refer students back to the work on stress in the previous unit. If necessary, produce a model sentence yourself, as you did before, in order to illustrate the point.

> But it articulates a be<u>lief</u> that was prevalent <u>then</u> and I think to some extent <u>still</u> is <u>now</u>. You can <u>either</u> be a normal woman <u>or</u> you can be a good scientist, but you can't possibly be <u>both</u>.

5.2
> **a** In each sentence, she stresses words with opposite meaning, e.g. *then* vs. *now* and *either* vs. *both*.
> **b** highlight a contrast (between a 'normal' woman and a woman scientist)

6 Useful phrases

6.1 For this activity, it may be a more economical use of time to divide the group into four and ask each group to focus on one particular category. When the groups have finished, they can feed back to the rest of the class.

> **Category A:** 1, 7
> **Category B:** 2, 3
> **Category C:** 5, 8
> **Category D:** 4, 6

> **Optional extension**
>
> PHOTOCOPIABLE
> Matching sentences page 116 (instructions page 105)

6.2
> **1** the whole point of
> **2** in the course of

Follow-up

7 Further research

7.1 For this activity, warn students against using Wikipedia and encourage them to use both paper-based and electronic media/research. Ask students to compile an annotated bibliography for the sources that they have referred to, so as to explain how they have used them and why they are helpful.

8 Further listening

8.1 B.4 In advance of starting this activity, draw students' attention to how they have developed the key skills in this unit for each of the pieces of information or examples they are looking for. If necessary, link each of the bulleted items to an exercise in this section.

5 On budget

Getting started

1 Goals, objectives and budgets

1.1 To focus students on this topic, ask them to think about how they spend their money and make it last throughout a term or semester. Divide the class into small groups and ask them to think about a typical student's expenditure and the different areas that it might be divided into. Once they have completed this exercise from a student's perspective, ask them to consider the budgetary area for a business. What differences are there?

1.2 👥 For the discussion section, prepare shyer students to ask follow-up questions by acting out the situation with a confident student in the class. You ask the student the question and then follow up to model the situation. This might work out as follows:

Teacher: *How easy do you find it to manage money?*
Student: *Quite easy.*
Teacher: *Can you explain a little more? What makes it easy for you?*

Reading

2 Reading for key information and concepts

2.1 👥 To add a fun element to this activity, give students a time limit and make the exercise a competition. Divide the class into pairs and encourage them to identify the two groups of words as quickly as possible.

> **a** Group 1 adjectives: broad, long-term, main, major, overall, primary, short-term, ultimate
> Group 2 verbs: achieve, determine, fulfil, pursue, set, work towards
>
> **b** target

2.2 Students sort the adjectives into two groups of four.

> Group 1: main, ultimate, major, primary
> Group 2: overall, long-term, short-term, broad

2.3a **Optional lead-in**

> Before embarking on this activity, refer students back to the verbs in **2.1a** and ask them to create some sentences. This should familiarise them with the vocabulary before using it in context.

Refer students to the rubric for this activity and encourage them to see how the verbs from **2.1a** will fit in.

beginning of the …	while doing the …	end of the …
determine	*work towards*	*achieve*
set	*pursue*	*fulfil*

2.3b 👥 In order to understand the usage of both the words in each sentence, ask students to work in pairs to discuss the differences in meaning. If dictionaries are available, invite the pairs to check the meaning of each pair of words and to refer to any example sentences in the dictionary. Explain to students that, where possible, they will be asked to explain their answer when they feed back to the class.

> **1** set
> **2** long-term
> **3** primary
> **4** achieve
> **5** set

2.4 Encourage students to analyse the assignment and to divide it into different sections to ensure that they answer each part appropriately. Explain that splitting out elements of the assignment and highlighting key words can help to focus. The following example may help:

Part 1 – What is a budget?

Part 2 – How is a budget different from a business objective?

> They both use examples.

2.5 👤/👥 In order to help students to use the texts and their knowledge of the key points required from the questions, ask them first to look at each set of questions and to be sure what kind of information they are looking for. They can do this either individually or in pairs. When this stage is complete, ask each student or pair to go through the text from the beginning, systematically answering one question after another. Remind them that sets of questions like this usually ask for information which appears in the text in the same order as the questions. It is rare for the last question to refer to the beginning of the text.

> **Text 1**
> 1 They will have financial consequences.
> 2 income and spending
> 3 organised or relaxed
> 4 all departments, including production, marketing, sales, research, design
>
> **Text 2**
> 5 A long-term plan can be for five years, while a budget is for a 12-month period. A budget is planned in relation to the long-term objective.
> 6 income, expenses, credit, staffing
> 7 a successful career that is rewarding

2.6 Before embarking on this activity, ask the class to volunteer their existing understanding of what a noun is. See how this compares to the definition in the Student's Book.

> **a** analogy
> **b** analogous
> **c** a budget

3 Grammar in context: expressing different levels of certainty

3.1 To start off the thought process and activate the relevant schema, turn the three areas of meaning into spider diagrams and ask students to brainstorm phrases or vocabulary which collocate or connect.

Write the suggestions on the board. The one for *obligation* might look something like the following:

> **a** possibility
> **b** 1 no   2 no

3.2 Before starting this task, check students' understanding of the function of modal verbs. Begin by asking for volunteers to provide a definition, which you can write on the board. Before you move on to the activity, make sure students understand that modal verbs are a category of verbs including *will*, *can*, *may* and *might*, and are used to describe different levels of certainty.

> **a** a 2, 4   b 5   c 1   d 3
> **b** 1 could   2 perhaps   3 that
> **c** 2 may have / might have / could have
>   3 is likely
>   4 may/might/could
>   5 may/might/could
>   6 may/might/could

3.3 To prepare for this activity, ask students to think of all the modal verbs they have encountered so far in the exercises in this unit. Ask the class to suggest words while you write them on the board. This list should then be useful for the exercises that follow, where modals need to be identified and underlined.

> **a** 1 … managers are human and <u>might</u> have different motives from the organisations they work for.
>   2 A large company <u>may</u> be able to undertake high-risk projects …
>   3 However, a major drawback of using cost centres is that managers <u>can</u> affect the amount of sales revenues …
>   4 … this <u>could</u> have a negative impact on staff motivation, as it would remove a great deal of variety … (NB *would* doesn't denote possibility)
>   5 … income is falling. This <u>may</u> have a negative effect on performance …
>   6 The additional income <u>could</u> help extend the product range.
>   7 Similarly, this <u>might</u> avoid the creation of queues, which are more stressful to customers …
>   8 Finally, a budget <u>can</u> encourage inefficiency and conflict between managers.
>
> **b** 1 could, can
>   2 b
>   3 Examples 3 and 8, both of which include *can* In the examples with *can*, the information is a little more certain.

3.4 This exercise focuses on the word *whether* and the expression of possibilities. Start off by clarifying the differences between the two homophones *whether* and *weather*. To ensure that students are aware of the different usage of these words, ask them to write some example sentences.

To test the validity of the rules, ask students to create sentences to see if the rule is true. This could be done in pairs or groups, and the different rules could be shared amongst the class in order to save time. Look at the two words in bold from the example taken from text 1.

> **a** possibilities
> **b** **1** a full clause
> **2** yes; yes
> **3** *or*
> **4** yes
> **c** Rule 2 is not correct.

4 Vocabulary in context: language to define terms

4.1

> **Optional lead-in**
>
> As this unit refers to a number of parts of speech, it may be useful to test students' knowledge of the terminology for this by creating a puzzle or crossword. Numerous downloadable activities can be found online if you type 'parts of speech crossword' into a search engine.

Divide the class into teams and first ask them to identify the different parts of speech in the sentence and the grammatical function of each element.

This may result in the identification of nouns and verbs, along with the subject and object of the phrase. It will be useful to explain that, although verbs sometimes appear as single words, a verb phrase using more than one verb can provide the same function.

> is called

4.2a

> **1** known, defined, called
> **2** is, are
> **3** as

4.2b Before students complete this exercise, explain that it is not important to understand exactly what each term means.

> **a** lexical check
> **b** recession
> **c** cognitive-behavioural therapy (CBT)
> **d** system of cities
> **e** contract compliance
> **f** the Year 2000 problem
> **g** low income
> **h** meteoroids

4.2c 👥 For this activity, encourage pairs of students to review the unit before they complete the rules. Then ask them to compare their completed rules with those of other pairs, and to test them by seeing if the rules actually do apply in example sentences.

> **1** *is*/*are* + *called* + new term
>   *is*/*are* + *known* + *as* + new term
> **2** *is*/*are* + *defined* + *as* + definition/ explanation

4.2d 1: something previously mentioned

> **Focus on your subject**
>
> This is a useful opportunity to introduce an element of subject specificity into the classroom. If possible, group students according to their area of academic focus, as they are likely to choose similar examples and may be able to learn from each other.

> **Optional extension**
>
> `PHOTOCOPIABLE`
>
> Guessing words through clues page 117 (instructions page 105)

Listening and speaking

5 Describing a process in a seminar presentation

5.1a

> **Optional lead-in**
>
> The topic in the listening for this section will deal with budgets, a theme which was introduced earlier in this unit. To help students focus, ask them to think about the challenges of budgeting and finance which might present themselves to people and communities in poorer countries.

👥👥 The questions for discussion could be divided amongst three groups in the class. Each group could then hold a mini-debate. Nominate a chair for each group and a person who will feed back on the main arguments which were raised.

5.1b Give students ten minutes to look at the questions and encourage them to discuss the meaning of any key vocabulary, before they consider the actual answers to the questions.

> **1** a
> **2** c
> **3** b

5.2 ◀)**5.1**

> **b** **1** budgeting in larger companies
> **2** yes
> **3** no

5.3 (◄)5.2

> Correct order: **2** F **3** A **4** E **5** G
> **6** B **7** D

5.4 (◄)5.3 This activity could be assisted if you have access to a language lab, so that students can focus and listen without external interference. If a language lab is not available, then students who wish to listen more closely could be given the chance to have a further individual hearing of the text through headphones in the classroom.

> **a** In this presen<u>ta</u>tion / I'd like to talk about the <u>way</u> the process of <u>bud</u>geting is put into <u>prac</u>tice / in a very par<u>ti</u>cular <u>con</u>text in the developing world. / I'll <u>start</u> by <u>brief</u>ly <u>summ</u>arising the way budgeting is <u>done</u> in <u>large com</u>panies. / Then I'll ex<u>plain</u> how this works in the de<u>vel</u>oping <u>world</u> with the <u>mi</u>crofinancing of <u>low</u>-income <u>peo</u>ple who want to <u>start</u> a <u>bus</u>iness. / After <u>that</u>, we'll look at what it <u>means</u> to create a <u>bud</u>get in this <u>con</u>text. / We'll then <u>move</u> on to <u>give</u> some spe<u>cif</u>ic ex<u>am</u>ples of how this has <u>worked</u> / and <u>fin</u>ish by evaluating the suc<u>cess</u> of the <u>pro</u>cess.
> **b** content words
> **c** **1** talk about, summarising, explain, look at, evaluating
> **2** start, move on to, finish

6 Giving a presentation: describing a process

6.1 (◄)5.2 Students need to listen for particular phrases that describe a process. This can be made into a bingo-like activity, and students can be divided into pairs or teams to encourage a competitive element. The main section of the presentation starts from (◄)5.2 1' 28" so you may wish to play the audio from here onwards.

> **a** **1** a
> **2** a
> **3** b
> **4** b
> **5** a
> **b** yes

6.2 If there is time, encourage students to produce a poster which they can describe to the class, focusing on the key process that they have identified.

Writing

7 Drafting and revising content

7.1 In this section, an essay title is introduced. Encourage students to draw on the material which has been provided in the form of texts and Kirsty's presentation,

but remind them to focus only on what is pertinent.

> **a** The initial references to big business won't be relevant to the essay.
> **b** microfinance, poverty, developing world

7.2 The first two paragraphs contain information that is similar to the presentation, but the remaining paragraphs don't. In these paragraphs, the historical background of microfinancing is described, and a disagreement on how to define microfinance is signalled.

> **Note**
> It is common for written texts to contain more information than spoken texts such as presentations.

7.3 Remind students that they are looking for specific information in this exercise, so they need to be sure that they understand the question before they refer back to the text for the required information.

> **1** They offer training in financial management.
> **2** in the 1980s
> **3** Social help aims to reduce poverty.

7.4 Explain to students that the three questions that Kirsty asks herself are intended to keep her on track and to answer the question in the essay title as accurately as possible. It is important not to waste words or time on anything irrelevant and to be as clear and precise as possible.

> **1** poverty
> **2** No, paragraph 3 doesn't.
> **3** social help

> **a** Yes, it does.
> **b** **1** definitions by where the poor live
> **2** absolute definition
> **3** by situation
> **c** **1** basic **2** less **3** standards **4** security
> **5** little **6** crowded
> **d** This paragraph should come after the second paragraph.
> **e** See the model answer on page 54.

7.6 The following example paragraph could be added to the second-to-last paragraph.
Gulli (1998) described one approach to microfinance that involves providing financial services that are sustainable. This is known as the 'financial systems' approach, and he indicates that if loans are paid back, then the service is useful. By contrast, the 'poverty lending' approach does not consider sustainability as important and it has the aim of reducing poverty so that people have control over their lives.

Grammar and vocabulary

- Words associated with planning
- Language of possibility
- Definitions
- Language of presentations
- Word families from the Academic Word List

1 Words associated with planning

1.1

Optional lead-in

Encourage students first of all to follow their instincts and then to check the usage of each word in the dictionary so that they can understand the appropriate contexts for the use of both vocabulary items or phrases.

2 determine
3 primary
4 working towards
5 achieved
6 main

1.2
Encourage students to think carefully about the sentences they write about their own learning. This exercise is useful, as it both uses the vocabulary from this section and focuses students on their own learning situation.

2 Language of possibility

2.1
This section revises the work completed on expressing possibilities and is a good test of understanding how to use the vocabulary that has been introduced.

1 Maybe we will get an increase in our student allowance next year.
2 Cuts in spending might be introduced.
3 An economic downturn can lower mortgage interest rates.
4 The department may exceed its budget this financial year.
5 Income from sales might increase by five per cent.
6 It's likely (that) they'll reach their investment target in the next three years.
7 A larger loan could allow these companies to expand abroad.

2.3

1 The economy **may / might / can / could / is likely to** improve next year.
2 The survey shows that many companies **may / might / can / could / are likely to** lay off five staff.
3 Internet marketing **may / might / can / could / is likely to** increase sales by as much as 20%.
4 Creating a budget **may / might / can / could / is likely to** help solve financial problems.
5 An increase in sales **may / might / can / could / is likely to** have a positive effect on staff motivation.

3 Definitions

3.1

Optional lead-in

Before completing this activity, you could draw on students' current understanding by listing the vocabulary on the left and asking them to provide their own definitions. This will make the matching activity much simpler.

1 d   2 a   3 e   4 b   5 c

3.2
Suggested answers
1 A broad objective is usually defined as a long-term goal that is not too specific.
2 A short-term financial plan is commonly known as a budget.
3 Budgeting is commonly defined as the process of creating annual financial targets.
4 The money a person or business earns is usually known as income.
5 Credit is usually defined as paying for something at a later time.

4 Language of presentations

4.1
For this task, encourage students to think back to the language used in the listening extract from Kirsty's presentation.

2 I'll start by ~~give~~ **giving**
3 ~~firstly~~ **first** of all
4 we'll see ~~at~~ **that**
5 How **do** we decide?
6 I'd like to talk about
7 we'll then move ~~in~~ **on**

4.2

1 I'd like to talk about
2 I'll start by giving
3 then I'll move on
4 we'll see that
5 We'll then move on
6 first of all
7 How do we decide

5 Word families from the Academic Word List

5.1

a sustainable (adj) – able to continue over a period of time [*CALD*]

b sustain (v), sustainability (n), sustained (adj)

c **1** sustain **2** sustainable **3** sustainability **4** sustain **5** sustained

d

Verb and meaning	Adjective forms	Noun form
constrain *Meaning:* to control or limit something*	**3** constrained **4** constraining	**10** constraint
maintain *Meaning:* to continue to have; to keep in existence or not allow to become less*	**5** maintained **6** maintaining	**11** maintenance
restrain *Meaning:* to control the actions or behaviour of someone by force, especially in order to stop them from doing something or to limit the growth of something*	**7** restrained **8** restraining	**12** restraint

* from the *CALD*

5.2

This section refers to collocation, which may not be a familiar term to students. Explain that collocation describes the tendency for certain words to occur side by side. For example, the words *sustainable* and *development* collocate.

2 financial constraint
3 maintain links
4 regular maintenance
5 considerable restraint
6 show restraint
7 sustain interest
8 sustainable development

5.3

2 constrained
3 maintained
4 restraint
5 Sustainability
6 restrained
7 constrain
8 maintenance

5.4

1 (business) plan
2 severely
3 (high) standards
4 practise(d)
5 growth
6 approach
7 spending
8 (close) ties

7.5e Model answer

It is also important to define exactly what poverty is in order to understand why microfinance is needed. Kotler and Lee (2009) define poor people as those who have an income level that does not allow them to meet their basic needs. They also outline three specific and different ways of defining poverty. Firstly, they mention the World Bank's 2005 definition of people who earn less than $1.25 per day. Secondly, the poor are defined by the United Nations as those people who have a standard of living that does not provide them with basic human rights associated with access to resources, choices and security. Finally, Kotler and Lee indicate that poor people can be defined by the place where they live. People who live in areas with little agriculture and industry are known as 'village poor'. People who live in the country but have economic problems as a result of natural disasters such as floods or droughts are known as 'rural poor'. People who live in crowded and dirty parts of a city are known as 'urban poor'.

6 Being objective

Unit aims

READING
· Close reading for key ideas
· Analysing information in more complex texts
· Grammar in context: modal expressions
· Grammar in context: relative clauses

LISTENING AND SPEAKING
· Agreeing and disagreeing

WRITING
· Paraphrasing information for essays
· Avoiding plagiarism
· Linking words 2

Getting started

1 Watching television and the news

1.1

Optional lead-in

In order to introduce this topic, ask students to think about their television viewing habits, both at present and when they are at home with their families. Their current circumstances may mean that they don't have access to a TV. Ask them how many hours per day they usually watch TV and how many channels they have access to. Ask what sort of TV programmes they prefer to watch. This could be organised in the form of a class poll or survey.

👥 / 👥👥 Ask students to work in pairs or groups to rank the different types of programme and their popularity in question 2. Ask them to think of why these particular types of programme are so popular.

For question 5, there is likely to be a variety of responses, but at least some class members should suggest that not all media reporting is objective. Use this to introduce the idea of objectivity and the fact that different perspectives often need to be evaluated.

> **2** Correct order: national/local news (69%), films (66%), comedy programmes (58%), live sport (52%), wildlife programmes (51%)
>
> Information taken from: http://www.statistics. gov.uk/downloads/theme_social/Social_ Trends39/Social_Trends_39.pdf p.194 table 13.3

Optional extension

It may also be useful to pre-teach the following words: *news reporter / journalist*, *news editor*, *cameraman*, *newsreader*. The following gap-fill task could be provided to check understanding:

Complete these job descriptions using the job titles.
A **1** _____ goes in search of news stories. He or she is filmed by a **2** _____ and the report is sent to a **3** _____ , who decides what stories will be included in a news programme. A **4** _____ presents the news programme to television viewers.

Answers
1 news reporter / journalist
2 cameraman
3 news editor
4 newsreader

Reading

2 Close reading for key ideas

2.1 In this section, the essay title about framing the news is introduced. Ask students if they can recall any examples from their own experience where 'framing the news' has taken place.

Note

In some cultures, the press and the government are closely connected, and if the particular culture does not respect criticism of the state, this topic may need to be handled delicately or perhaps with references to international broadcasting corporations such as the BBC or CNN.

After the class has read the text, ask them if they think 'framing the news' is an ethical activity.

Context 2

2.2
1 relevant
2 interpret
3 perspective

2.3
1 framing in real life
2 taking a photograph
3 what a journalist reports

2.4

> **Paragraph 1:** 1
> **Paragraph 2:** 3
> **Paragraph 3:** 6

2.5 For this activity, students need to read the details for each paragraph carefully. They should check their comprehension and then try to find the corresponding passage in the text. Explain that they then need to work through a process of elimination. Don't provide any more structure at this stage, as this will follow in **2.6**.

> **a** **Paragraph 1:** explain
> **Paragraph 2:** we include people or not
> **Paragraph 3:** they use different language for
> different stories
>
> **b** definitions

2.6

> **1** Because it provides a definition of a key term and it is important to have an in-depth understanding of the concept.
> **2** Step b) is not appropriate because it focuses on what students (or readers) don't know, rather than working from a base of what they can understand.

2.7 As well as looking at the dictionary definitions as provided in the Student's Book, encourage students to look in their own dictionaries or online via the Cambridge online dictionary resources to see where the definitions are similar or different.

> **a** no
> **b** The meaning in the text is closest to meaning 1 in the dictionary. However, the dictionary meaning is neutral, whereas the meaning in the text gives the concept of 'framing' a negative connotation. This more negative meaning is linked to media studies.

Listening and speaking

3 Agreeing and disagreeing

3.1 In this section, students will be practising discussions and agreeing and disagreeing. You can help them to prepare for this by staging a short discussion with one of the more confident members of your group. Ask them for an opinion on something which has taken place recently in the news or in your school or neighbourhood. You can then demonstrate agreement by responding and using agreement or disagreement strategies such as:

I see what you mean!

I agree with the point you made about …

I'm afraid I don't really agree with that.

3.2a 🔊 **6.1**

> Ewa – Student A
> Millie – Student B
> Pablo – Student C

3.2b 🔊 **6.1** For this activity, tell students that you will allow them to listen twice and that the first time they listen, they might like to use note form. The second time they listen, they can write full phrases. Explain that this is a good method to follow, as they might struggle to keep up to speed if they try to listen and write at the same time. Of course, note-taking is also a useful practice in other contexts, such as lectures.

> See audioscript on pages 159–160.

3.3 Students consolidate their answers to **3.2b** by completing the table.

Agreement	Part agreement	Disagreement
2 I couldn't agree more.	**3** I can see what you mean, but … **4** Yes and no. **5** Well, I sort of agree with that. **6** Yeah, but …	**7** I'm afraid I don't really agree with either of you. **8** Do you really think so? **9** Yeah, but there's something else … **10** I really don't accept that argument. **11** Well, it's not a question of …

Optional extension

PHOTOCOPIABLE

Discussing academic questions page 118 (instructions page 106)

Focus on your subject

This a very useful opportunity to discuss an area associated with students' academic specialism. If you have a group with areas of shared specialism, then the opportunities for authentic subject-related discussion and the use of agreement and disagreement will be extended. If your class has mixed specialisms, you could invite them to discuss which subject area makes the most important contribution to society.

Reading

4 Analysing information in more complex texts

4.1 As an introduction to the text, ask students to describe the ways in which TV news is generally presented. What are the common features, and which tools or props help to set the scene?

> Yes, the excerpt talks about the 'look and sound' of TV news.

4.2
> **1** voice-over
> **2** reaffirmed
> **3** address 'dialogic'
> **4** integrity
> **5** trustworthiness
> **6** upholding

4.3 Encourage students not to use the dictionary at this stage, but rather to guess the meaning. The aim is to focus as much as possible on what students can understand from the text rather than any vocabulary which they are unfamiliar with.

> **a** **a** address
> **b** upholding
> **c** trustworthiness
> **d** dialogic
> **e** integrity
> **f** voice-over
> **g** reaffirmed
> **b** integrity

4.4
> Sentence 2

5 Grammar in context: modal expressions

5.1 This next section once again refers to verb phrases, along with possibility and obligation. Refer students back to the previous unit, where this was focused on. Remind students that a verb phrase is often the predicate of a sentence. The predicate gives details about the subject, such as what the subject is doing or what features the subject has.

> **1+2** appear(s) to, seem(s) to (possibility)
> is / are to be (obligation)
> **3** appear(s) to, seem(s) to
> **4** c, f, h: *must* replaces *is/are to*, but not the verb *be*

5.2 👥 Students work in pairs to complete the rules. Then get them to test the rules by writing sentences which demonstrate the usage. They can compare notes with other pairs to check their understanding before feeding back to you.

> **1** *seem*
> **2** base
> **3** phrase
> **4** *are*
> **5** past

6 Grammar in context: relative clauses

6.1 In this section, students practise the use of relative clauses. Explain the use of relative clauses by writing the following information on the board:

Relative clauses give additional information. The information can either provide an important definition of something (defining clause) or just offer extra, but non-essential, details (non-defining clause).

Relative clauses are usually preceded by:
- a relative pronoun: *which*, *that*, *whose* or *who* (*whom*)
- no relative pronoun
- *who*, *where*, *why* or *when* in place of a relative pronoun

> **a** **1** institution
> **2** It refers to *institution*.
> **3** which
> **4** that
> **5** the subject

> **b** **1** The British broadcasting organisation <u>that is most well known</u> is the BBC.
> **2** John Logie Baird, <u>who invented a mechanical TV</u>, created a television line system used by the BBC in the 1930s.
> **3** The TV channel <u>that I usually watch when I'm travelling</u> is BBC News.
> **4** The woman <u>who we were introduced to</u> is a famous journalist.
> **5** Television, <u>which is often considered one of the most controversial inventions of the 20th century</u>, completely changed people's leisure time from the 1950s onwards.
> **6** The journalist <u>that they spoke to</u> reported the information incorrectly.
> **c** **1** 1, 2, 5
> **2** 3, 4, 6
> **3** subject; object
> **4** yes

6.2 👥 This activity is a rule-building task. See how much students already know and encourage pairs to write their own set of rules without looking at the Student's Book. When they have finished, get the pairs to stand up and circulate around the room collecting rules from other pairs. The aim is to build a larger set of rules for the use of relative clauses through comparing notes with the rest of the class. When they have collected all the rules, select one pair to read out the full list for checking.

When this is finished, the exercise in the Student's Book will be simpler to complete.

> **a 1** T   **2** F (They are always subordinate.)
>   **3** T   **4** T   **5** T   **6** T
> **b 1** who/that
>   **2** which
>   **3** which/that

Writing

7 Paraphrasing information for essays

7.1
> **Optional lead-in**
>
> The series of activities in this part of the unit focuses on plagiarism avoidance, which is a key skill for students to understand and acquire. It is important to realise that attitudes towards what constitutes plagiarism differ from culture to culture, as approaches to academic writing also depend on the culture in which they are located. Take the opportunity to refer students to your institutional rules on plagiarism, and warn them about the penalties that are imposed if plagiarism is detected. If your institution uses plagiarism detection software such as Turnitin, then this would also be a good opportunity to introduce that.

As paraphrasing is a useful tool for plagiarism avoidance, ask students what the word means; if they are unsure, set them a quest to find a definition in a dictionary or online.

Just before they report back on the definition, tell them that they cannot define the word using the same words which they found on the Web or in the dictionary – they have to use their own words to show what they have understood. This will solicit an understanding of both the theory and practice behind paraphrase.

> He should explain the ideas in his own words, i.e. paraphrase the text (see next task).

7.2
> Correct order: d, f, a, c, b, e

7.3
> **a** the kind of music used to introduce the news
> **b** a general statement
> **c 1** newsreaders   **2** viewers   **3** strategy
>   **4** conversation   **5** pay more attention to
> **d** ... that TV channels try to have ...
>   ... which means the viewer will pay more attention to the news story ...

7.4
> Suggested answer
> The final point that Allan makes is the way that newsreaders dress and use gesture can make them seem like an important person. As a result, (or This can mean that) viewers are more likely to trust what newsreaders say and believe that the information is both truthful and reliable.

8 Avoiding plagiarism

8.1 🔊6.2 Before playing the recording, ask students to discuss their experiences of plagiarism in the past and whether they or a friend have ever made a mistake which has been considered to be plagiarism. What did they do to avoid making the same mistake in future?

> **1** Maria discusses plagiarism.
> **2** Maria – making writing clear and factual, hedging language for claims, referencing appropriately
>   Zaneta – understanding and implementing a correct structure for different genre, time management of writing, different countries (cultures) having different rhetorical patterns
> **3** Zaneta found that writing got easier with practice.

9 Linking words 2

9.1 Encourage students to read the text for gist and to focus on meaning rather than any gaps in their understanding.

Before embarking on this exercise, explain to students that linking expressions help to connect different phrases or sentences together. They also help with sequencing and order, showing how one element flows on or is joined to the previous part.

> **1** T
> **2** F
> **3** T
> **4** T

Explain also that connectives can often be divided into different categories such as reason, result, adding information (e.g. *also* or *besides*), comparing and contrasting.

9.2

1 so
2 As a result,
3 who
4 This can mean that
5 so
6 This is the reason that
7 which
8 Consequently,

9.3

a

Result	Reason	Relative pronoun
so; consequently; as a result	this can mean that; this is the reason that	that; who; which

b 1 all except *so* and the relative pronouns
   2 *so* and the relative pronouns

9.4

2 A recent survey indicated that most people get their news from TV or the Internet. ~~so~~ **However**, a surprisingly large number of people prefer to get their news from the radio.
3 Many newspaper websites include all articles from their print edition so readers can choose how they get their news. ✓
4 The *Guardian*, a well-established British newspaper, also has a very good website. ✓
5 Accessing newspaper articles online is now very common. However, many people still prefer to read a print edition of a newspaper because they say that they find it easier to read. ✓
6 There is often a lot of advertising in the middle of TV news programmes. ~~So~~ **Consequently / As a result**, many people choose to record the news and press 'fast forward' during the advertising breaks.
7 Journalists sometimes get their information from public relations companies ~~who~~ **which** represent large companies. This can mean that 'the news' is not really objective even before they write the story.
8 Boris, ~~which~~ **who** is studying to become a journalist, has won a scholarship to a university in Australia.

9.5 👥 Books closed. Ask students to think about how the paragraphs could be linked. From the work already covered, which connectives and joining phrases would be most suitable?

When students have given this some thought, ask them to open their books and choose the best sentence from the two provided. Make sure they are prepared to justify their answers.

a Sentence 1 links paragraphs 2 and 3; sentence 2 links paragraphs 1 and 2.
b Sentence 1, because it uses the linking phrase *the final tool*. The word *tool* links back to the ideas in the previous paragraph, and the word *final* introduces the fact that the writer is coming to the end of a list of ideas.

9.6 See the model answer on page 62.

Grammar and vocabulary

- Verb and noun collocations
- Language of agreement
- Modal expressions
- Relative clauses
- Linking words and phrases

1 Verb and noun collocations

1.1 This activity refers back to verb phrases. It may be necessary to review this section from earlier on in this unit. To check that students still understand what verb phrases are, ask them to look at a passage from an article or book you are using in class and to identify verb phrases and how they are constructed.

> focusing on

1.2
> 1 a picture
> 2 a conference
> 4 a lecture
> 5 prices
> 6 a committee
> 7 irrelevant information

1.3
> 2 ~~selected~~ organised
> 3 ~~focus~~ aspects
> 4 ~~organised~~ frozen
> 5 ~~categorised~~ selected
> 6 ~~select~~ exclude
> 7 ~~exclude~~ frame
> 8 ~~froze~~ categorised
> 9 ~~select~~ pay attention
> 10 ~~frame~~ select

2 Language of agreement

2.1 Before embarking on this exercise, you can help students tune back in to the idea of collocation by playing a quick game. Make a list of adjectives, nouns and verbs from this unit and add some others which are relevant to students' study context(s). Divide the class into two teams and tell them that points will be awarded for shouting out words which go together (or collocate) with the words you read out. For example, if you read out the word *news*, a student might shout out the word *bulletin* or *story*. For *TV*, students might respond with *show* or *viewers*.

> agreement: 4 + 6
> part agreement: 1 + 3
> disagreement: 2 + 5

2.2
> 1 phrase 2 or 5
> 2 phrase 1 or 3
> 3 phrase 4 or 6
> 4 phrase 1 or 3
> 5 phrase 2 or 5
> 6 phrase 1 or 3

3 Modal expressions

3.1 Before starting this exercise, ask students to remind you what a verb phrase is. If necessary, write a sentence on the board and ask them to identify the verb phrase.

> 1 This news story ***appears to*/ *seems to*** have been edited to make viewers sympathise with the government.
> 2 News editors agreed that all stories ***are to be*** written in a neutral tone.
> 3 The newsreader's authority ***appears to* / *seems to*** have been relaxed a little as a result of a more casual style of dress.
> 4 Journalists usually feel strongly that everything they film ***is to be*** shown on the evening news. However, news editors often disagree.
> 5 There ***appears to* / *seems to*** have been an increase in the amount of live reporting in order to make the news seem more up-to-date.

4 Relative clauses

4.1 This exercise practises relative clauses and goes over the difference between defining and non-defining clauses. Make sure that students are fully aware of how the use of commas plays a crucial role.

> 1 who (add commas)
> 2 that/which
> 3 who
> 4 which (add commas)
> 5 who (add commas)

4.2
> 1 which
> 2 no pronoun necessary
> 3 who
> 4 no pronoun necessary
> 5 which/that
> 6 no pronoun necessary

4.3
> **Optional lead-in**
>
> To show how relative clauses perform a joining function, write two sentences on the board and demonstrate how they can be connected in this manner.

> **1** Al Jazeera is an international television network (that is) based in Doha, Qatar.
> **2** It was the first international TV network that broadcasts in Arabic.
> **3** The second channel that Al Jazeera set up in 2006 broadcasts in English.
> **4** The journalists that Al Jazeera has employed for its English-language channel come from all over the world.
> **5** Many viewers throughout the world believe Al Jazeera represents a point of view that is an alternative to other international TV networks.

5 Linking words and phrases

5.1 👤 / 👥 Ask students to complete this exercise individually and then compare their results with a partner. If they finish quickly, ask the pairs to think of possible synonyms or alternatives for the correct joining expressions that they have selected from the box.

> **2** However
> **3** so / which means
> **4** Furthermore
> **5** This can mean that
> **6** this can mean that / so / as a result
> **7** Consequently
> **8** Furthermore
> **9** However
> **10** so / which means

Model answer

9.6 Model answer

The final tool that is used in television news journalism is the presentation or packaging of news. Production values such as camera movement, studio design and the quality of the newsreader's voice are used to make the news appear to be more personal. Television newsreaders who make eye contact with the camera are able to get the viewers' attention. As a result, the news is similar to a conversation, which means television viewers feel it is more personal. The clothes that they wear and the gestures they use can also make newsreaders seem important. Consequently, viewers trust what newsreaders say, and the news seems to be more truthful and reliable.

Lecture skills C

Preparing for lectures

> **Note**
>
> Before engaging students with this unit, check that they have fully understood the material from Lecture skills B.

1 Chemical elements

1.1 👥 Organise students into pairs for this activity and if they are not sure of the answers, ask them to check in a dictionary, where the entries for the chemical symbols should also be included.

You can also direct students to the website http://www.chemicalelements.com, which includes a useful interactive tool to help remember symbols for the periodic table of elements.

> **b** **1** h **2** g **3** a **4** i **5** e **6** c
> **7** j **8** d **9** b **10** f

2 Predicting information from visuals

2.1 Explain to students that the aim of this exercise is to get them thinking about context and imagery in the slides. If students are focused on the topic, they will be better prepared for the listening activity. The questions in the Student's Book are intended to encourage students to think about the different people in the slides. Draw students' attention to the study tip on page 95 of the Student's Book. The photocopiable slides at the back of this Teacher's Book (pages 127–128) can also be used in similar preparation activities.

3 Vocabulary for the context

3.1 Before they use a dictionary, ask students to go through the list of words in a small group to see how many they are already familiar with and if they can use the words in sentences.

> **b** **1** methodical **2** spectacular **3** contribution
> **4** revolutionary **5** responsible **6** glamorous

> **Background information**
>
> *The following background information may be useful for some students:*
>
> In the lecture, Dr Fara refers to two institutions: *the Metropolitan in New York* and *Cornell in America*.
>
> *The Metropolitan* is the Metropolitan Museum of Art in New York. This is where the painting of Antoine and Marie Lavoisier can be seen.
>
> *Cornell* is Cornell University, a private university in Ithaca, New York. This is where some of Marie Lavoisier's drawings can be found.

> **Optional extension**
>
> **PHOTOCOPIABLE**
>
> Generating new language page 119 (instructions page 106)

Listening

4 Listening for gist and detail

4.1 🔊 **c.1** To encourage listening for gist, tell students in advance that one of them will be asked to give a gist summary to the rest of the class. This will assist in focusing their attention on the activity.

Ask groups of students to compare their own descriptions with those in the extract. What are the similarities and differences?

> **2 a** T **b** F

4.2 `C.1`

> **a+b** Correct order; suggested extra notes in bold
> **2** Antoine Lavoisier (AL) makes important contribution to science
> **revolutionises chemistry – introduces chemical symbols used today**
> **3** painting suggests AL is only person responsible
> **instruments on table – AL writing in the book**
> **4** folder contains ML's drawings
> **ML was art student under painter David**
> **5** ML draws picture of laboratory
> **different from public image in painting**
> **6** In drawing, AL looks like a stage director
> **has a team of people working for him**
> **7** Marie Lavoisier (ML) writes measurements in notebooks
> **her responsibility as well as organising the workshop**
> **8** ML studies English when she marries AL (13 years)
> **AL never learned English**
> **9** ML translates from English to French for AL
> **translates textbooks and research papers**
> **10** AL's textbook includes illustrations of instruments
> **also detailed instructions of how to make instruments**
> **11** ML drew all textbook illustrations
> **careful and accurate illustrations**
> **12** ML receives no credit for her work
> **but very important in AL's work**

Language focus

5 Language for focusing on visuals

5.1 `C.2` This question requires students to identify key information, as it is sometimes important to pick out particular pieces of information. You may need to play the recording more than once if students do not catch the missing words the first time.

> **Extract 1**
> … and you **can see here** this side of the picture, the **right-hand** side of the picture is his side …
>
> **Extract 2**
> But **if you look** in that folder, which you **can just see** on the left of the picture, that's a folder of her drawings …
>
> **Extract 3**
> And it **presents** a very different image from the public one **I've just showed**[*] you.

> **Language note**
> Dr Fara says: 'And it presents a very different image from the public one I've just showed[*] you.' We would normally say: '… I've just **shown** you.'

5.2 In the three excerpts, Dr Fara is asking students to look at the slides and focus on specific aspects of them. The language in the excerpts aims to draw students' attention to visual information.

6 Beginnings and endings

6.1 She is making a point in both extracts.

6.2 `C.3`

> **b 1** But
> **2** yet
> **c** contrasting ideas

7 Intonation

7.1 `C.4` For this section, it may be very useful for you to model certain sentences as used in the extract so that students can hear some of the intonation features more clearly.

> … and you can see here, this side of the
>
> picture, the right-hand side of the picture, is his ↘ ↗
> side. All the instruments are **there**. He's writing ↗
> the revolutionary **book** that was to go out all ↗
> through the **world**. Erm, and he's – so he is solely
>
> responsible according to this official picture for ↘
> the instruments in the **book**. And he's gazing up ↗ ↗
> at his **wife** who's propped up on his **shoulder**, er, ↗ ↗
> Marie **Lavoisier**, looking incredibly **glamorous**,
>
> obviously spent hours in the hairdresser getting ↗
> ready for this **picture**. Obviously got nothing to do ↘
> with **science**.

7.2 `C.5`

> **a** Her tone is lower.
> **b** It is extra information that might be of interest to people listening.

Follow-up

8 Critical thinking

8.1 In order to encourage further thought on the topic of genius, you might like to ask students to look at the definitions provided on this website: http://www.theabsolute.net/minefield/genqtpg.html. This will further fuel their critical thinking on this subject.

8.2 | See the model answer on page 66.

9 Further listening

9.1 **C.6** If students are interested in learning more about women in science, additional video and presentation material can be found on YouTube. Just type 'Women in science' into the search engine.

Model answer

8.2 Model answer

Dr Fara makes the point that, in the past, the idea of 'genius' is associated more with creative artists such as painters, musicians and poets because their works were often a result of a flash of inspiration. In contrast, scientists discovered ideas as a result of on-going, methodical work. In the 19th century, this view changed, and scientists were seen as more inspirational and more like geniuses when compared to inventors. The reason for this is that scientists did their work because they wanted to understand the truth of what they studied and they were not interested in making money as inventors were. Nowadays, businessmen such as Bill Gates are seen as geniuses because of their ability to make money. As a result, Dr Fara suggests that our view of the idea of genius in relation to different professions has changed over time.

 Lecture skills C

7 Innovation

Unit aims

WRITING
- Paraphrasing by using synonyms
- Grammar in context: comparing and contrasting

READING
- Approaches to note-taking 2

LISTENING AND SPEAKING
- Turn-taking in discussions

Getting started

1 New ideas

1.1 In order to focus students on the situation, ask them to discuss which item of technology they couldn't live without. Typically this might be their laptop or mobile phone. Ask for reasons that explain why the features are so useful for them, and how the technology may have improved in recent years. Encourage students to think about innovation, as this will feed into their understanding of the text.

1.2 ▌It explains the concept of innovation.

1.3 👥 Before looking in the dictionary, ask pairs to look at the word *innovate* and to guess what they think the different forms in the word family will be. Ask them if the ending reminds them of any other verbs that they are familiar with. This is a good way to get students to draw on their existing knowledge of word forms and patterns.

▌**a 1** innovate   **2** innovative   **3** innovator

Note

See the Grammar and vocabulary section for extra practice.

Writing

2 Paraphrasing by using synonyms

2.1 👤 / 👥 Before answering the questions which relate to the essay title, ask students to read the title individually. They should then highlight the various sections of the title and make a list of the different things that they have to do when writing the essay. Once they have written a list, students work in pairs to discuss what they think they will have to do. This will be good preparation for answering the questions.

> **a 1** good
> **2** not good: The focus of the essay should be on countries, not individual companies.
> **3** good
> **4** not good: It would be better to take a limited number of countries and discuss these in detail rather than try and review a large number of countries.
> **5** good
> **6** not good: It will be necessary to include some facts and figures to support arguments.
> **7** good
> **b** He doesn't focus on the idea of competition signalled in the essay title. He could make a note to himself about including an example of two countries in competition in an area of innovation.

Optional extension

PHOTOCOPIABLE

Thinking about synonyms page 120 (instructions page 107)

2.2 👥 To help students to think about the topic further, write the question *What is innovation?* on the board and ask them to discuss this in pairs. This will prepare them well for the text and accompanying questions.

a 1 No, she believes it also occurs between nations.
  2 No, she lists different factors: education and training, research and development, government policies, etc.
  3 research and development
b 1 She believes it is the result of people working in contexts – *both organizational and geographical.*
  2 It created a national system that encouraged innovation.
  3 It allowed the country to become a leader in a flexible approach to manufacturing.
  4 It also helps economic growth.
c The following points are relevant for Jun's essay:
  – Business innovation often comes out of a national context that helps creative individuals / companies.
  – A national system (or strategy) that focuses on factors such as training and R&D helps innovation – a good example is post-war Japan.
  – Investment on a national level as well as from individual companies helps the economic growth of a country.

2.3 For this activity, it will be necessary, first of all, to check students' understanding of what a synonym is. Illustrate the point by acting out a short role-play. Pick a student and tell them that they need to respond to each comment that you make using a word which means *good*. Tell the student that they can't actually use the word *good*, but rather they need to use a different word for every response that they give. For your part of the dialogue, make statements which could receive a positive response such as these:

Teacher: *I have just booked a holiday in France.*

Student: *Excellent!*

Teacher: *I am really looking forward to it.*

Student: *Great!*

Teacher: *I can't wait to have some free time.*

Student: *Wonderful!*

When you have finished, explain to students that the words used by the student are all synonyms, and that the variety adds interest, as using the same word continually would be repetitive. Clarify also that using synonyms can help us to personalise the language that we use.

a 4 b
  5 d
  6 h
  7 i
  8 a
  9 e

b 2 improvement in technology
  3 creative individuals and companies
  4 are different from
  5 colleagues and competitors.
  6 work in specific places
  7 in organizations and countries
  8 have an important role
  9 and developing creativity
c 1 c
  2 a
  3 b

Refer students back to Unit 6, where the concept of paraphrasing was introduced. Explain that using synonyms is also part of paraphrasing. Make it clear that it is important that the original meaning is retained, so synonyms need to be chosen carefully.

2.4 For this exercise, it may be useful to refer students to a thesaurus. You could also use the online resources available at http://dictionary.cambridge.org. Explain to students that it is important, however, not to overuse a thesaurus and to check that the original meaning has not been lost.

See the model answer on page 74.

3   Grammar in context: comparing and contrasting

3.1 Before they look at the questions for this exercise, ask students to work in pairs and to look at the bar chart. Ask them to think about the information that they can see and what the chart demonstrates. Give the pairs five minutes to discuss it before they feed back to the class.

a 1 1975 and 2006
  2 Switzerland
  3 Sweden
  4 Finland
  5 the Czech Republic, Poland, the Slovak Republic
  6 Switzerland and the US / the Czech Republic and Spain / Poland and the Slovak Republic

3.2 Refer students to the key patterns and trends which are highlighted in Jun's summary. Encourage them to add any further statements they identified which might be missing from Jun's version.

The following questions from **3.1** are mentioned in the summary: 1, 3, 4 and 5.

3.3

a+b

	One syllable	Two or more syllables	Irregular
Comparative adjectives	great → greater big → bigger long → longer small → smaller	notable → more notable interesting → more interesting substantial → more substantial	bad → worse far → farther/further good → better
Superlative adjectives	large → largest big → biggest long → longest small → smallest	significant → most significant interesting → most interesting substantial → most substantial	bad → worst far → farthest/furthest good → best

c 1 than
  2 the
d 1 less
  2 a noun
  3 an adjective
  4 yes

3.4 For this task, explain to students that you are practising the language of comparing and contrasting. As a pre-activity, refer them back to the passage written by Jun and ask them to identify and underline comparing and contrasting phrases.

a 1 to
  2 in
  3 contrast
  4 made
  5 between
  6 in
b 1 years
  2 countries
  3 years
  4 countries
  5 countries
  6 countries

> **Note**
> See the Grammar and vocabulary section for extra practice.

3.5 To focus students on this activity, refer them back to the sentences in **3.4a** and challenge them to remodel the sentences based on the content of this new chart, but to try and use the same structures for comparing and contrasting.

b 2 In contrast
  3 more
  4 compared
  5 larger
  6 in relation to
  7 the difference between
  8 In contrast
  9 largest
  10 compared

> **Focus on your subject**
> 👥 Make sure you take advantage of this section to encourage students to compare and contrast aspects of their own academic area of study. It may be useful to have groups work together who are focused on the same area of study.

Reading

4 Approaches to note-taking 2

> **Note**
> As this section refers to social innovation, it may be useful to ask students to think of any projects they may be aware of from their own cultures which might provide relevant examples. If students are interested in learning more about this topic, you could also refer them to this website:
> http://www.socialinnovationexchange.org/node/97

4.1 It may be useful to give students some ideas to illustrate the kind of examples you are thinking of. You could provide a model by using the UK or the US as an example and listing some common problems and examples of social innovation.

4.2 👥 Looking at the seminar discussion topic, ask students how comfortable they would be discussing this subject at present. It is unlikely that they will feel very able to discuss the topic; explain that this is why preparation and background reading are so important. Emphasise that it is normal to feel daunted when presented with a new topic, and that they should think of reading as helpful rather than extra work, as it can help open up a topic and make it more accessible.

4.3 Point out that the noun *entrepreneurship* refers to the activity rather than a person.

Although the activity requires students to fill in the grid after reading the text, you can test students' existing knowledge by seeing if they can attempt to fill in the table for social entrepreneurship before reading the text. This will also help them to focus on the gaps in their knowledge when they start reading.

> Yes, the text is useful for Jun to complete his note-taking table.
>
> | | Social entrepreneurship |
> | --- | --- |
> | **Definition** | focus on social problems; aims to benefit society; works together with business |
> | **Example** | create park in industrial area; improve quality of local school |
> | **Entrepreneur role** | recognise opportunities to create social benefits; use available resources; feel responsible towards people |
> | **Kind of person** | like change; sometimes immigrants; many are first-born children; people who feel restless |

4.4 For this activity, make sure students realise the importance of understanding words in context. Explain that the words which surround a vocabulary item and the type of text have an important effect on the meaning of a word. If necessary, refer students to an entry for a word in a dictionary and show them a list of different definitions.

> **a 1** *emerge* – verb – no
> **2** *noteworthy* – adjective – *note + worth*
> **3** *latent* – adjective – no
> **4** *accountable* – adjective – *account*
> **5** *innate* – adjective – because they're born with it
> **c 1** context
> **2** word building
> **3** context
> **4** word building
> **5** context

4.5 Explain the concept of gist to students and help them to see that by understanding the general meaning of this text, it can help to unlock meaning and information which can be used for other purposes. Jun needs to understand the text, but probably not to the same level of detail as required for an essay.

> Option 3

Listening and speaking

5 Turn-taking in discussions

5.1 ◀)7.1 👥 In order to get students thinking about this activity, ask them to discuss in pairs if they agree with the information in the text. This will activate their thinking process in preparation for the listening activity.

> **a** Gillian agrees more.
> **b** Gillian's main point is that seeing community workers as social entrepreneurs makes them seem more professional.
> Jun's main point is that giving them this title can make them seem uncaring.

5.2 ◀)7.2 To start this exercise, draw a table on the board showing that you are going to compare and contrast social entrepreneurship with business entrepreneurship. Ask the class to think of ways in which they are similar and different, based on what they have already read. Then move on to the listening exercises.

> **a 1** Peter
> **2** Francesca and Gillian
> **3** Jun
> **b 1** She suggests that the role of social entrepreneur makes the job sound more interesting and positive.
> **2** Peter thinks the language is positive, but it doesn't have a lot of meaning for him.
> **3** Yes, she does.
> **4** They both have goals that they want to achieve.
> **5** Commercial entrepreneurs want to make money, but social entrepreneurs want to create social value.
> **6** See answer for **5.3**.

5.3 ◀)7.3

> Jun says he found it difficult to know when to take a turn in the discussion.

5.4 The questions in this section get students to think about their own experiences in discussions and in particular in turn-taking. Ask students to think about different situations, such as talking to friends and talking in seminars, and encourage them to draw on different experiences. See if they experience a similar lack of confidence in their first language(s), or whether it is the challenge of communicating in English which affects their communication skills.

5.5

a 1 What do you guys think?
   2 that's just my opinion
   3 yeah
   4 having the same goal

b 1 inviting a comment: *What?, Isn't that right?,
   ... would it make you want to become a 'social
   entrepreneur'?, So what else have they got in
   common?, Jun, what do you think?*
   2 phrase/expression to indicate speaker has
   finished: *That's my idea.*
   3 vague word: *but still ..., ... you know.*
   4 Gillian (fifth speech) repeats Peter's idea on
   money or social value.

5.6 For the discussion activity, it may be useful to
divide groups into two and to encourage the different
parts of the group to argue along different lines.
This will ensure that the discussion is lively. Before
practising the turn-taking strategies, ask students
to go through each strategy and confirm their
understanding. This will be a useful and safe way to
check comprehension before moving into the group
discussion. It will also be a good idea to nominate
one student as the chair for the discussion, so that all
students can be encouraged to contribute.

5.7 Although the summary report can be set as a
homework task, encourage students to make their
notes straight away while the discussion is still fresh
in their minds.

Grammar and vocabulary

- *Innovation* word family
- Synonyms
- Comparative language
- Articles
- Joining ideas

1   *Innovation* word family

1.1 Before going through this activity, ask students to look
at the list of words, which clearly come from the same
base. Ask them to label each word with its correct
word form. Before looking at the sentences that follow,
you could also check their skill in usage by asking
them to make their own sentences with each of the
words.

   1 innovative
   2 innovator
   3 innovation
   4 innovate
   5 innovation

2   Synonyms

2.1 Check students' understanding of the role of
synonyms and that they have grasped the importance
of using words in context and not overusing a
thesaurus.

   2 signal
   3 helps
   4 development
   5 illustrated
   6 spheres
   7 most important
   8 notably

2.2 As an initial activity, go through the words in the
box in **2.1** and allocate each word to a different pair
in the class. Ask them to identify different possible
word forms from the vocabulary item that they have
been allocated. This will help in preparation for the
questions that follow.

   2 illustrated
   3 companies
   4 notably
   5 signal
   6 most important
   7 help
   8 sphere

3 Comparative language

3.1
2 more substantial
3 longest
4 more interesting
5 more doubtful
6 shorter

3.2
1 interest
2 expensive
3 worried
4 significant
5 doubt

3.3
1 In contrast, the UK spent much more in 2006 than in 1975.
2 Germany spent more on R&D in relation to the UK in 2006.
3 When the comparison is made, the Czech Republic spent more on R&D than Poland in 2006.
4 The difference between the Czech Republic and Spain in R&D spending is not significant.
5 Germany spent more on R&D in 2006 compared to 1975.

4 Articles

4.1 Before you set students to work on this activity, ask them to work in pairs to write two or three model sentences which use the definite and indefinite article. While students are doing this, ask one or two pairs to include sentences which contain an article where it is not needed. When students are ready, go through the sentences and write them on the board. Next, ask students to try to identify some patterns of usage and to spot the sentences that use articles incorrectly, where in fact no article is needed at all.

a a zero article
b indefinite article
c definite article
d definite article
b 1 c **2** a **3** b **4** d

4.2
2 ✗
3 a
4 ✗
5 a
6 ✗
7 The
8 the
9 the
10 the
11 ✗

5 Joining ideas

5.1 For this activity on clauses, first close books and ask students to recall the work they completed on different types of clause in Unit 2. Build up a set of ideas on the board. This work on the board should help students when it comes to answering the questions.

1 T
2 T
3 F (It can also be a noun phrase.)
4 F (Not all verbs (intransitive ones) require an object.)
5 T

5.2 Ask students to use highlighter pens or different colours to mark the different clauses in the sentences. Make sure they are able to explain their answers, rather than just guessing.

a two main clauses
b 1 and **2** but **3** or
But comes after a comma.

5.3 Refer students to the board work completed in **5.1** and their knowledge from Unit 2. This activity will probably work best in pairs.

1 clauses
2-4 and, but, or
5 middle

Optional extension

Write a paragraph that describes the information in this bar chart. Use language that compares and contrasts.

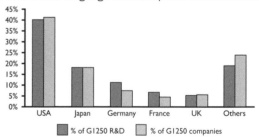

The distribution of R&D expenditure among the top 1,250 companies in the world most active in R&D in 2006
from: www.innovation.gov.uk

5.4 This exercise involves the use of conjunctions to make two sentences into one with multiple clauses. Check that students understand the joining function of conjunctions and ask them to write a model sentence which shows how a conjunction is used.

1 Social entrepreneurs want to help people in the community **and** they want to improve the quality of life for everyone in a city.
2 Social entrepreneurs are usually very caring people, **but** they have a very business-like approach to solving social problems.
3 Social entrepreneurs try to fix social problems **or** they try to meet the needs of a specific community.
4 Many people might want to get rid of an old house that is falling down, **but** a social entrepreneur might see this house as an opportunity for a community centre.
5 Social entrepreneurs sometimes come from immigrant families **or** they might be the first-born in a family.

Model answer

2.4 Model answer

Morrison goes on to say that nations can play a particularly important role in developing new technologies. This idea shows why Japan was so successful in the 1980s in developing new technologies that improved the way goods were manufactured. A country can help create innovation capacity in a variety of ways, such as making sure the workforce is well educated and trained, carrying out R&D, planning the financing of research, having up-to-date telecommunications and encouraging co-operation between companies.

8 Sensing and understanding

Unit aims

READING
- Text organisation 1
- Grammar in context: passive constructions
- Vocabulary in context: word building

LISTENING AND SPEAKING
- Signposting in seminar presentations
- Giving a presentation

WRITING
- Linking words 3
- Grammar in context: using the passive to manage information in texts

Getting started

1 Describing images

Optional lead-in

👥👥👥 Books closed. Use your computer or a book from the library to show students a series of images of well-known works of art. It might be useful to choose pictures from artists such as Monet and Van Gogh, so that they are familiar to students. If you have access to the Internet, you may prefer to display a series of images directly from the search results screen, rather than going to individual websites.

When you have an image ready on the screen or in a book, ask the group to describe what they can see. At this stage, don't worry about particular phrases for describing. Use this activity to familiarise students with the description process. You'll also get a good idea of the group's strengths and weaknesses.

1.1a 👥👥👥 Ask the two groups to look at their respective pictures, and encourage them to describe what they see. Suggest that students talk about the following aspects of each work of art: the material it is made from, the age it comes from, what they think it means, etc. You could ask some of the following questions as prompts:

What can you see?

What is shown in the image?

Which different elements or parts do you notice?

What can you see in the top, bottom and middle?

What is happening in the image?

What type of art is it?

What colours are there?

How was the artwork made?

Is it modern or old?

1.1b 👥👥 In order to build students' confidence for this task, you may like to give an example description of one of the images you found on the Internet in the Optional lead-in for this section. Use the expressions provided in the Student's Book to describe one of the images and see if students can guess the image that you are talking about.

If you have a very confident student, you can ask them to repeat the activity with a different picture, demonstrating again how to describe using the expressions given.

Once you have provided a satisfactory model, ask students to take it in turns to describe their image without showing it to their partner.

> The second image is of a sculpture and is likely to be seen in a museum or art gallery. The first picture might also be seen there, but it is a poster and so a reproduction could be seen in a print shop.

1.2a 👥👥 Ask the pairs to explain whether the image matches the description that they were provided with: in what ways does the image differ from the description, and how is it similar? Encourage students to work together to provide a more accurate description of each image.

1.2b This activity requires students to categorise the artworks according to the type of art that they fall into. This may be a useful point to introduce some of the following vocabulary items and to check students' comprehension. You could even write the words on the board and ask for definitions or provide time for dictionary use:

drawing, sketch, oil painting, watercolour, photograph, canvas, sculpture, carving, collage, installation, abstract, figurative

> 1 Group B's picture (page 112)
> 2 Group A's picture (page 111)
> 3 Both images are figurative.
> 4 It's a carving (on the doors of a Norwegian church).

1.3a
1 line
2 form
3 pattern
4 design
5 figure

1.3b Once students have identified which image can be described using which words, ask them to suggest sentences that use these words in descriptions. This will show that they can use the words, as well as identify their context.

> John Alcorn drawing (page 111): line, figure, design
> Giacometti statue (page 112): line, figure, form
> Carved doors (page 110): design, line, pattern

Reading

2 Text organisation 1

2.1 After reading the essay title, focus students on the topic by asking them to explain how different artists that they know have used a particular medium to express themselves. As an example, you could explain how Van Gogh used rich patterns and texture in oil painting in order to convey passion, depth and vibrancy. For this exercise, it may be useful to refer students to a dictionary for a definition of the word *value*. This will help them to see the different meanings in different contexts.

> **a 1** b
> **2** b
> **3** a
> **b 1** It includes a quote from another source.
> **2** Eight elements are mentioned. NB Some elements contain two words, e.g. *shape* and *form*.
> **3** only one

2.2
> The best summary is 2; however, as well as identifying this summary as the most accurate, ask students to justify their reasoning. They should go back through the text and highlight the points which have led them to this conclusion.

2.3 👥 / 👥👥 Students can discuss their ideas in pairs or groups. Get feedback from the whole class once they have had a chance to exchange views.

2.4 This exercise involves taking notes, so it will be useful to refer students back to Units 3 and 7. Ask them to remind you of the strategies which they have already learned.

Students may also need reminding about useful note-taking symbols and abbreviations. Pick out three from Ania's notes (for example =, → and *vs.*) and check that students understand what they mean.

The exercise uses a kind of framework, so explain to students that they will need to use scanning techniques in their second reading of the extract to fill in the missing information.

> **2** Japan, China
> **3** see at a distance
> **4** drawing for *The Scarlet Letter* on TV
> **5** positive/filled space
> **6** Norwegian door panels
> **7** the shape to animals into snakes and then into plants
> **8** of inter-connected lines
> **9** *Walking Man*
> **10** isolation and loneliness of individual
> **11** empty space around figure

2.5
> **1** c
> **2** yes
> **3** You could use this pattern for descriptive texts or texts that make a general point followed by more detail. These kinds of texts are said to follow a general–particular text pattern.

3 Grammar in context: passive constructions

3.1 In this section, students are introduced to the passive voice. As a result, it will be useful to show them some general examples of the passive and active voices in action in more everyday contexts. You could use the classroom and the situation around you to provide a model for these. For example, hold up a book and say *John Smith wrote this book*. Then hold up the same book and say *This book was written by John Smith*. Ask students to consider the difference in emphasis in the two sentences and explain how the focus has shifted from the subject to the object.

> **a 1** past time
> **2** no
> **3** yes, a craftsman
> **4** The first phrase is passive and does not indicate the person or thing that carried out the action, while the second example is active and we know who carried out the action.
> **b 1** Both contain a modal verb: *may* in the first example and *can* in the second.
> **2** Example c
> **3** Example c
> **4** Example d

3.2

> **Optional lead-in**
>
> 👥 Books closed. Before completing the grammar rule, ask pairs to discuss and formulate a rule in their own words for the use of the passive voice. Ask pairs to read out their rules to the class. Write them on the board and discuss their validity together.

Ask the same pairs to fill in the missing words in the text and, when they have finished, to compare their results with another pair in the class.

2 action
3 passive
4 know
5 agent
6 passive
7 active

3.3 🧑 Ask students to work through the text individually and to underline the verb forms which they think fit the sentence most effectively. Before you discuss the answers with them, ask individuals to compare their answers in pairs and to justify why they have made their decisions.

1 are not physically created
2 are suggested
3 are sent
4 perceive
5 are drawn
6 have been left out
7 is given

4 Vocabulary in context: word building

4.1 Books closed. This exercise introduces the different meanings of the word *perceive*, so after students have identified this vocabulary item as the common factor, ask them to use their dictionaries in order to find the different definitions which relate to this word.

perceive

4.2 **a** Definition 1: 3, 4
Definition 2 is incorrect.
Definition 3: 1, 2, 5
b Definition 3

Listening and speaking

5 Signposting in seminar presentations

5.1 In preparation for the listening and speaking activities, activate students' vocabulary by asking them to think of words associated with seeing and perceiving.

You can also use the images in this section as a springboard. In the same manner as a brainstorming activity, write the words *seeing* and *perceiving* on the board and ask students to suggest other words which are connected with them.

Once you have built up a series of associated words, ask students to make some example sentences using one or more of the words provided.

◀)8.1 Before students listen to the extract, ask them to read through the two summary sentences and to speculate on which they think is likely to be correct. Remind them that this type of exercise is similar to a scanning activity in reading, as they are listening for some specific details.

Summary 2

> **Optional extension**
>
> PHOTOCOPIABLE
> An art presentation page 121 (instructions page 108).

5.2 Correct order: **1** C **2** D **3** A **4** E **5** D **6** B

5.3 ◀)8.2

1 So **having looked at** the way our environment provides us with a lot of visual information, **I'd now like to move on to** explaining …
2 **What I mean is** what goes on in our eyes and our brains …
3 OK, so **if we now look at** this diagram of an eye ….
4 … here's our lamp, or **should I say** here's the image of the lamp, but it's upside down.
5 So **coming back to** our diagram of the eye …
6 So **now let's** look at how our brain makes sense …

5.4 👥 In pairs, students sort the expressions into the table provided. As they allocate each expression to a category, encourage them to write a sentence using the expression in another context that they are familiar with.

After students have classified the expressions using the table, ask pairs to write a model dialogue of their own, showing how the expressions can be used in other contexts. Once the dialogues are ready, check the work of each pair. This will help to highlight the transferability of this type of language, and will also help to build confidence for the oral-presentation exercise that follows.

a	Expressions used to refer to slides	Expressions used to show a change in topic	Expressions used to explain something more clearly
	3, 5	1, 6	2, 4

b 2 forward
  3 getting
  4 focus
  5 should I say
  6 returning to

5.5 This exercise will draw on students' understanding of the use of the expressions and will demonstrate the extent to which they have understood the topic. Encourage students to structure their presentation by using the slides appropriately. They will be able to use the expressions that they have been practising, along with the key points which they have retained from the listening activity.

Focus on your subject

This activity is an extremely useful opportunity to get students to see the relevance of the language they have learned to their particular subject context. The process of seeing has been the topic used in this section of the book, but try to get students to think of a process which is important in their field. It might help if you keep a list of students' subject specialisms so that you can prepare a few suggestions for the class in advance, in case they struggle for inspiration. Alternatively, students can use a hobby that they know a lot about for their presentation subject.

6 Giving a presentation

6.1 ◀)8.3 Before you ask the class to listen again, ask them to reflect on their previous experiences of giving a presentation. Get them to explain to each other how it felt and which elements of the process they found the most challenging.

The following tips were given:
Fei – prepare enough material, structure the presentation carefully, decide on key points in the presentation, use PowerPoint
Maria – use PowerPoint, don't try to memorise the whole presentation, be friendly, try to get meaning or main ideas across, try to make it entertaining and keep it brief
Frederike – don't be afraid, she suggests that your language doesn't need to be perfect (appropriate), it will get easier
Frederike found that it got easier.

Writing

7 Linking words 3

7.1 First, ask students to reflect on the key points which were raised in Tim's presentation on perception. If necessary, students can then look at the audioscript to make sure that they have gleaned all the necessary information for comparison purposes. Once students are confident that they have fully understood the presentation, ask them to read the text and to note any additional information.

New information in the text:
a person has the ability to perceive many different things; an action that is known as 'attended stimulus'; we are able to make sense of what we looked at. This results in what Goldstein calls 'conscious sensory perception'

7.2 As preparation for the activity on linking expressions, ask students to reflect on the work which has been completed in previous units on connectives. If necessary, revisit previous units to revise the work done.

Before giving students the answer to the rule in **7.2d**, encourage pairs to discuss their answers and to suggest a supporting rationale.

a First of all, While, As soon as, The next step, After, Finally
b 1 When
  2 Secondly,
  3 Following this, / After this/that,
  4 Following this, / After this/that,
  5 Lastly,
  In addition and during cannot be used.
c during
d These sequencing discourse markers are usually placed at the beginning of a sentence.

Optional extension

To demonstrate the fact that sequencing markers are usually placed at the beginning of the sentence, write a series of example sentences on the board, some of which incorrectly position sequencing markers in places other than at the beginning of a sentence. Ask students to identify and correct problematic sentences.

8 Grammar in context: using the passive to manage information in texts

8.1a If necessary, in advance of this activity, refer students again to the differences between active and passive voice and the rationale for using the passive in academic writing. It is particularly important that they are aware of why the passive is a key feature of academic writing.

> The writing is better in Tim's version.

8.1b 👥 Students work through the second version of the text systematically, in pairs, and underline and identify the examples which relate to the problems listed.

> 1 **We** know this process as transduction …
> … **we** create new electrical signals in nerve cells …
> **We** call these nerve cells neurons …
> … **we** are able to make sense of what we looked at.
> 2 As soon as the receptors react to the **pattern of light**, something transforms the **pattern of light** …
> … in **nerve cells** that are connected to the brain. We call these **nerve cells** …
> 3 As soon as the receptors react to the pattern of light, **something** transforms the pattern of light …
> … in a more general sense, means that **something** transforms one kind of energy into another kind of energy.
> After they get there, **something** transforms the signals once more into the experience of seeing …
> 4 … are connected to the **brain**. We call these **nerve cells** …
> … a series of complicated **pathways** between our bodies and our brains. The **electrical signals** travel …

8.2 Students need to draw on their understanding of the passive voice and problems in academic writing that passive structures can help us to avoid. Refer them back to the problems that were listed in **8.1b**.

> 1 b
> 2 a
> 3 b
> 4 a
> 5 b
> 6 a

8.3 To prepare for this activity, revise the work in this unit on process descriptions and the correct usage of sequencing markers.

> 2 is collected
> 3 (is) sent
> 4 is converted
> 5 When / As soon as
> 6 are perceived
> 7 set
> 8 send
> 9 Next / Following this
> 10 stimulates
> 11 create
> 12 are picked up
> 13 are sent
> 14 Finally
> 15 interprets

8.4 👥 Ask students to work in groups for this activity and to nominate one group member who will read out the final process description to the class.

Explain again to students that the models for process description in this unit are a useful transferable skill area for the description of other processes in other academic contexts.

Refer groups back to any work they have completed in this unit relating to their own subject area, and encourage them to put together a process description which can be read out to the rest of the class, including appropriate sequencing markers. It may be useful to create new groups who share similar areas of subject specialism.

> See the model answer on page 82.

Grammar and vocabulary

- Art and design vocabulary
- Passive forms
- *Perceive* word family
- Signposting in seminar presentations
- Linking words

1 Art and design vocabulary

1.1

Optional lead-in

Before you ask students to start the gap-fill activity, divide the words which are provided across groups in the class and ask them to write as many short sentences as they can in five minutes using the words. After five minutes, ask each group to report back to the whole class. This will help the class understand how to use each of the words in different contexts. You can also repeat this activity for the new words, which are listed in **1.2**.

1 figures **2** texture **3** pattern **4** line **5** forms

1.2

1 form **2** line **3** texture **4** shape **5** space

2 Passive forms

2.1

To revise the usage of the passive voice, ask pairs to discuss the rules that they can remember and to explain them to another pair. This will be a useful preparation for filling in the table. Write or project the table onto the board and ask students to come to the front and fill in the missing items.

1 are **2** was **3** may / might **4** be **5** seen

2.2

Refer students back to exercises earlier in the unit on the passive and active voices and try to make sure that they are aware of the function as well as the form before they embark upon this exercise. Ask for a rationale for each answer provided.

2 painted
3 shows
4 are/were used
5 was influenced
6 created; painted
7 was taken
8 were designed

2.3

The exercises completed in earlier sections of this unit provide all the guidance required for the completion of this activity. Ask students to identify the previous activities which are relevant, so that they can use these to help find the answers to the questions.

a 1 verbs
  2 perceive
  3 No, because there is no noun or pronoun that follows it that can become the subject of a passive sentence.
b 1 noun **2** object **3** both **4** not
c 2 T **3** T **4** I **5** I **6** T **7** T

3 *Perceive* word family

3.1

a 1 perception (n)
  2 perception (n)
  3 perceptible (adj)
  4 perceptive (adj)
b Definition 1: 2 and 3
  Definition 2: 1 and 4
c having a good understanding; insightful

Optional extension

This exercise focuses on word families and uses *perceive* as the vehicle for this. If you would like to extend the exercise or provide a context which is relevant to other disciplines, choose an alternative word family and ask students to create a series of different sentences.

You could allocate different words from a word family to different groups, or challenge pairs to come up with as many words as they can in a particular family. The groups or pairs should then put their words into their own sentences.

3.2

If there are some students who are still struggling with using the correct parts of speech in the correct position in the sentences, encourage them to check the words that they need in a dictionary. They should also examine the words both before and after the gap in order to help guess which form is required.

1 perception
2 perceive
3 perceptible
4 perceptive

4 Signposting in seminar presentations

4.1 Before moving ahead with the exercise on signposting, ask students to explain their understanding before they proceed. Elicit from them that the role of the words and phrases used is to highlight sequencing and processes. Remind them of the processes that were described earlier in the unit.

> 1 having looked **at**
> 2 I'd like to **move** on
> 3 if we now **look** at
> 4 now let's focus **on**
> 5 **what** I mean by doing this
> 6 returning **to**

5 Linking words

5.1

> **Optional extension**
>
> ⚑ To check comprehension and to stretch students' vocabulary, ask them to work in groups to think of alternative linking expressions which might act as synonyms for the words in this activity.

> 1 First of all
> 2 In addition
> 3 After this
> 4 During
> 5 Finally

Model answer

8.4 Model answer

When we smell something, odour chemicals in the air reach our nostrils. First of all, these chemicals are dissolved in mucus, which is found inside each nostril. Next, special receptor cells in our nostrils detect the odour and send this information to the olfactory bulb, which then sends a message to the brain. When the brain receives this information, the odour is perceived.

 Unit 8 | Sensing and understanding

Lecture skills D

PREPARING FOR LECTURES
· Discussion on global warming
· Vocabulary for the context
· Predicting

LISTENING
· Listening for gist and detail

LANGUAGE FOCUS
· Referring words
· Emphasising structures

FOLLOW-UP
· Taking action
· Further listening

Background information

This section focuses on global warming, and there is a wide range of material available to help prepare students for dealing with this theme.

The following video produced by NASA Earth Science provides key facts on the subject and might act as a useful introductory medium:
http://www.youtube.com/watch?v=ROZJmX73FF4

Preparing for lectures

1 Discussion on global warming

1.1 In preparation for this exercise, ask students to discuss what they know about global warming and, if they watched the video in Background information above, to think of the key messages which they took from it.

> Suggested answers
> 1 It is widely believed that emissions of carbon dioxide contribute to global warming (also known as 'climate change'). However, some scientists and politicians dispute this and are known as 'climate change sceptics'. Their argument is that the changes in temperature are part of the Earth's natural temperature cycles.
> 2 Most commonly cited evidence of global warming is a rise in land and sea temperatures. The melting of polar ice caps and irregular weather patterns are also considered evidence.

> 3 All activities that involve burning fossil fuels, in particular oil and coal. This encompasses use of cars, flying, oil-fired heating systems and industrial production. Deforestation also contributes to CO_2 emissions because fewer trees mean that less CO_2 is absorbed from the Earth's atmosphere.

2 Vocabulary for the context

2.1 As preparation for this exercise, refer students back to the work in the earlier units which focused on noun phrases. Elicit some examples of noun phrases from students and ask them to explain their usage.

> sustainable energy, volcanic activity, water shortages, greenhouse gases, melting ice caps, crop failure

2.2
> 1 Greenhouse gases
> 2 volcanic activity
> 3 crop failure
> 4 melting ice caps
> 5 water shortages
> 6 sustainable energy

3 Predicting

3.1 This activity is similar to the prediction work undertaken in the previous unit. Students simply need to discuss their thoughts on what the pictures on the slides suggest to them. The aim is to start thinking about the field so that when they watch the lecture, the topic is already familiar.

> Suggested answers
> **Slide 1:** *This slide seems to show the relationship between* Europe and lights. The light looks brighter where there are cities. The map could represent energy use.
> **Slide 2:** *This slide looks like* a description of how global temperatures have changed since 1850 and how they are likely to change in the next 90 years.
> **Slide 3:** *This slide shows* the way in which the amount of CO_2 in the atmosphere has increased dramatically since the invention of the steam engine in 1769.

Optional extension

PHOTOCOPIABLE

Describing graphs page 122 (instructions page 108)

3.2 (D.1)

Optional lead-in

In order to illustrate the power of body language, ask students to watch and listen as you model an additional lecture extract of this same topic. You'll need to do this twice. You only need to speak for one or two sentences. In your first delivery, use no body language and the second time you deliver the same material, include some body language. Ask students if they felt that there was a noticeable difference.

1 Extract D – He looks directly at the audience and his head moves around the lecture theatre; he has a querulous expression on his face.

2 Extract C – He points more than once to the screen behind him which suggests he is reading out some kind of series.

3 Extract B – He is holding up an object (a brick) and referring to it as he speaks.

4 Extract A – His hand gestures upwards and then drops (almost in a circular motion).

Listening

4 Listening for gist and detail

4.1 (D.2) Remind students of the similarity between skimming and scanning, and gist and detailed listening, and make sure they understand when these different skills need to be used.

3 1 Extract 3
  2 Extract 1
  3 Extract 4
  4 Extract 2
4 Description a

4.2 (D.2)

1 CO_2	**5** water shortages	**9** 30	
2 sea level	**6** ice caps	**10** 100	
3 agriculture	**7** sea	**11** 2	
4 crop failure	**8** 2		

Language focus

5 Referring words

5.1 (D.3)

1 that's   **2** this   **3** this   **4** this

5.2 **a** 4   **b** 2, 3   **c** 1

6 Emphasising structures

6.1 (D.4)

a **Extract 1:** nice is
  Extract 2: extraordinary is
b **1** nice   **2** extraordinary

6.2 (D.4)

a 1 at the end   **2** 6.1a
b 1 The strongest stress is on the adjective.
  2 highlight
  3 rise
  4 more information will follow

Follow-up

7 Taking action

7.1

Optional extension

In support of this exercise, ask students to visit the following website, which allows you to calculate your carbon footprint and find ways of reducing it: www.energysavingtrust.org.uk

7.2

Optional extension

Set a reading activity for homework based on David J.C. MacKay's book, *Sustainable Energy – without the hot air*. You could choose a section that is particularly relevant and ask gist and/or more specific questions.

8 Further listening

8.1 (D.5) The graph is fairly complex, so it might be worth giving students a few minutes to look at it, to ensure they understand that the vertical axis shows levels of greenhouse-gas pollution and the horizontal axis shows population. You could then ask a few comprehension questions:

Which country produces the most greenhouse-gas pollution? (Australia)

Which country has the largest population? (China)

Which country produces a surprisingly high level of pollution compared to its population? (Qatar, United Arab Emirates)

9 IT issues

Unit aims

READING
· Text organisation 2
· Grammar in context: hedging language

LISTENING AND SPEAKING
· Problem–solution patterns and repair strategies

WRITING
· Generating ideas
· Grammar in context: cohesive devices
· In-text referencing

Getting started

1 Computer problems

1.1 Books closed. As an introduction to the topic of computers and IT, ask pairs to make a list of all the gadgets and computers that they and their friends and family own or use in their lives. When they have done this, ask them to describe any difficulties that could be caused by the use of computers and gadgets. If you would like to extend this further, ask students to fill in a grid like the one below, which lists positive and negative aspects of computers and computerised gadgets.

Positive and negative aspects of computers and computerised gadgets

Positive	Negative
They speed things up.	They might crash and lose information.

Make sure that you check the meanings of the words in bold in the sentences yourself, so that you are ready to answer any questions students may have. Some words (e.g. *phishing, cyberterrorism*) are peculiar to the IT lexis; others (e.g. *hack, spam, virus*) have specific meanings in this area.

1.2 This section involves the ranking of IT-related issues according to seriousness. It may be useful to go through each of the areas listed in advance so that students can discuss their understanding. The second bullet point may need to be described sensitively, according to the culture and religion of students. You might also like to guide students in the ranking process by suggesting they rank according to both legal and social difficulties that may be caused by the problems listed.

Answers will differ according to the individuals in the class, but before you feed back, it is probably useful to explain this so that the debate does not become too heated.

1.3 Before asking students to complete this exercise, explain that it is often easier to understand definitions of words from example sentences which can appear in dictionaries. Before looking at this example, show students some example sentences, either from the online dictionary or from paper copies that you have to hand. Choose an example that clearly helps in understanding the definition of a word.

> **a** honest
> **b** For the question associated with ethics, explain that ethicality can also change from person to person, not only from country to country.

Reading

2 Text organisation 2

2.1a To make this exercise more fun, you can split the analysis down and allocate the task to four different pairs or groups in the class. Ask one group to focus on underlining content words and each of the other groups to focus on one of the other three areas of analysis. When each group has finished, ask the groups to talk to at least one member from each of the other three groups until they have built up the full analysis by discussing how they separately marked up the essay title.

2.1b
1 No, because the title refers to issues that are both ethical and illegal. Therefore, it is possible to choose an issue that is unethical but not necessarily illegal, for example, using a fake identity on a social-networking site.
2 Yes, this would be a good way to introduce the issue that you eventually focus on.
3 Both, as well as anyone else that the issue affects, for example, people in the criminal justice system. The question mentions stakeholders, meaning anyone with an interest or anyone who is affected.
4 The essay title does not ask you to discuss the issue. It asks you to outline it and talk about the impact. Therefore, it is more likely to be an explanation/description rather than a discussion.

2.2
> The information is more likely to be used in an introductory section, because it is looking at crime in general rather than focusing on specific crime.

2.3a Remind students that a base word is a word to which prefixes or suffixes can be added in order to create related words. Encourage students to look inside the longer words listed here and to pick out shorter words which have had affixes joined onto them.

> **1** detect   **2** law   **3** legal   **4** report

If students need further support for this activity, encourage them to look the words up in a dictionary to see if any of the listed definitions or example sentences match or are similar to the definitions in this question.

2.3b
> **a** law   **b** report   **c** detect   **d** legal

2.3c
> **1** not
> **2** -ed: It shows that the word is either simple past or a past participle form; therefore, the words could either be verbs or adjectives.
> **3** unlaw<u>ful</u>
> **4** -ful indicates that the word is an adjective.

Optional extension

PHOTOCOPIABLE

Negative prefixes page 123 (instructions page 108)

2.4a As further guidance to students, copy the bullet points from the Student's Book onto the board and ask the group to give further examples of what the different parts of the process are likely to include or look like. Solicit ideas from students and mark up their comments so that it looks something like this:

– They describe a situation.

A situation is introduced or summarised.

A general picture or issue is described.

– They outline a problem associated with that situation.

Difficulties connected to the theme are introduced or discussed.

A more specific context or focus is explored.

– They indicate responses/solutions to the problem.

A series of possible ways of reacting or dealing with the difficult situation is provided.

A list of options to consider is offered.

– They evaluate the response/solution.

The writer considers which response might be best.

A comparison or contrast of relative merits is presented.

When you have finished and you are confident that students have a good understanding of what features they are looking for in the text, ask them to work through the text highlighting the different stages of problem-solving.

> **Paragraph A:** 1
> **Paragraph B:** 2
> **Paragraph C:** 3
> **Paragraph D:** 3
> **Paragraph E:** 4

2.4b With reference to the board work in **2.4a**, ask students to take notes that mark why each section corresponds to each of the stages of problem-solving.

> **Situation:** IT provides benefits, but can be unethical / unlawful; variety of computer crimes (cc) from theft to illegal copying
> **Problem:** cc serious – more money stolen than robberies; no exact idea of how much cc takes place
> **Response/Solution:** many cc reported, but not all prosecuted; not enough expertise in criminal justice system – cc often difficult to prove; business suffered less, but employees more of a problem than computer criminals; improved technology controls employee crime more
> **Evaluation:** cc recent, so justice system and businesses working hard to deal with it

3 Grammar in context: hedging language

3.1a Before students look for words to underline in this exercise, check that they understand what hedging means in this context. It is useful to make the distinction between the general English usage of the word and the use in this context, which refers to the use of intentionally non-committal or ambiguous language. Explain that hedging is a part of cautiousness to reduce any risk of making statements that may be inaccurate.

Explain the importance of hedging by comparing the risks and potential challenges that might be associated with these sentences:

The PC is the best invention in the world.

The PC is arguably the best invention in the world.

The PC is arguably one of the best inventions in the world.

2 While most of us <u>typically</u> associate computer crime with the theft of sensitive data …

3 <u>It is widely accepted that</u> computer crime is a serious problem …

4 <u>In principle</u>, the criminal justice system tries to deal with computer criminals.

5 Also, prosecutors <u>may</u> not be well prepared from a technical perspective to prosecute such cases.

6 <u>Seemingly</u>, business has suffered less than individuals as a result of IT and criminal activity.

7 <u>In general</u>, however, automatic processing provided by computer technology has improved controls and checks on employees …

8 <u>It is believed that</u> those in the criminal justice system need to develop more expertise …

1 ~~Most people I know say~~ **Broadly speaking**, the criminal justice system is effective at dealing with crime.

2 ~~There are quite a few people who sort of agree~~ **It is generally agreed** that fraud is the most common crime in the business world.

3 As a crime, credit card fraud ~~sort of~~ **probably** causes less physical harm to victims.

4 ~~More often than not~~ **In most cases**, longer prison sentences do not help reduce crime rates.

5 More education in sensible and safe credit-card use ~~is maybe going to~~ **could** reduce fraud.

Listening and speaking

4 Problem–solution patterns and repair strategies

4.1 (◄)9.1) 👥 / 👥👥 In preparation for the listening activity, explain to students that they are going to hear two people, Sally and Matteo, discussing the essay title and the work that they have been doing. To focus students, ask them to discuss in pairs or threes what Sally and Matteo might be talking about. The aim is simply to get students focusing on this kind of exercise before they start listening, so it doesn't really matter if the suggestions that they make are different from the true focus of the dialogue.

1 computer viruses

2 None – they are brainstorming before they begin reading.

3 No, they both use vocabulary that the other doesn't understand. This is more of a problem for Matteo.

4.2 (◄)9.1) 👥 Divide the class into pairs for this activity and give them a large piece of paper, possibly A3, to write their completed notes on. Tell them that they will be showing these notes to the rest of the class during this activity. Once each pair has completed and written up their notes, divide the class in two and nominate one pair in each group to lead the team in producing a single set of notes, based on the best elements of the pairs. When this is finished, compare the two sets of notes from the two teams and have the class vote on which is best.

3.1b If students have difficulty in understanding the terms for different grammar categories, refer them to one of the many resources on the Internet, such as http://www.iscribe.org/english/def.html. This provides a series of grammatical terms and their definitions.

Category	Example
Modal verb	may
Adverb on its own	typically, seemingly
Prepositional phrase	in principle, in general
It + passive construction	It is widely accepted that, It is believed that
Expression	generally speaking

3.2 👥 For this activity, students work in pairs so that they can compare their understanding whilst reflecting on the rules which are embedded within the examples provided in this unit. When each pair has finished completing the rules, ask them to work with another pair to check their answers. Warn each pair that they will need to be ready to give example sentences that illustrate each of the rules they have completed.

1 beginning

2 beginning; comma

3 after

4 *that*

3.3 If students need to check the formality or informality of a word or phrase, encourage them to look it up in a dictionary.

Suggested answers

Situation: different computer **viruses** and different **results**

Problem(s):
- lose all data
- **annoying** jokes
- spread **quickly**
- two main types: **computer worms and macro viruses**
- timing: **immediate and delayed**

Solutions:
- education and **informing everyone**
- **anti-virus software**
- **backing up**

Evaluation: difficult to **stop hackers – people need protection**

4.3a In Extract 1, Sally uses a phrase (*hit the books*) that Matteo doesn't understand, and in Extract 2, Matteo uses a false cognate (*disgrazia*) that doesn't make sense to Sally in the context of their conversation. In both cases, they need to explain the word or phrase.

Ask students for any other examples they may have experienced. If you need another example, a common false cognate for French and English speakers is *sympatique* ('kind' in French) and *sympathetic* ('understanding' in English).

4.3b Before continuing with **4.3b–d**, ask students to think about occasions where they have failed to make themselves understood, and what they have tried to do to get themselves out of any difficult situations.

> **2** c   **3** a   **4** b

4.3c   **a** 4   **b** 2   **c** 3

4.3d   **Extract 1:** I mean
Extract 2: it's like

4.4 Before asking students to look for further examples, try to get them to see the repairing function in the two extracts which are provided on pages 130–131 of the Student's Book.

> **a** Repair strategies are not always used when a speaker says a new word. In the first example listed in the next column, Matteo probably knows the word *joke*, but he is checking how it is being used in this context. In the second example, there is a pronunciation problem that requires repair. Example 3 is similar to example 1. In the final example, Sally is checking how broad the meaning of *education* is.
>
> **b** In each extract, the expression that introduces the clarification is underlined.

1 S: And there are the ones that are just jokes.
M: Joke? But it's not funny when you get a virus.
S: Yeah. No. It's not. <u>What I mean is</u> that all the virus does is create a silly message that appears on your computer screen. But that's all they do. You get the message or the joke or whatever and it's all over. They're harmless – they don't hurt anyone. But they can be annoying.
M: OK yes – now I get it – just a funny message.

2 M: Then there are the little ones, you know, called 'verms' …
S: Verm … ? Oh, do you …
M: <u>Yes, sorry</u>, 'worm'.
S: Yes, 'worm'.

3 S: Separate entities.
M: Yes. What? Separate en…?
S: Entity. <u>You know</u>, something that exists independently.
M: Entity.
S: Yeah.
M: Separate – on their own.

4 M: Education.
S: You mean at school?
M: <u>Yes, but also</u> educating and informing everyone – telling them all the time what they need to do. They need to be careful when they open unknown email and things like that.

Optional extension

If there is time, ask students to practise rephrasing sentences as a means of clarifying meaning. Choose a confident student from the group and ask them a question, as an example. When the student replies, ask them for clarification. Before they respond, make sure that they know that you want them to paraphrase their last response.

When you've done this and the rest of the class understands the model, students practise in pairs. Later, choose pairs to perform and illustrate the technique in front of the class.

4.5a 👥 If possible, pair confident students with less confident ones for this exercise. The activity of changing roles will help to embed the repair strategy and build confidence.

4.5b This clarification activity is a useful opportunity for students to talk about their subject specialisms. If possible, organise the class into pairs, each of whom specialises in a different academic field.

Writing

5 Generating ideas

5.1a Refer students back to other situations in this book where they have been encouraged to start thinking about a topic as a means of stimulating ideas.

> Thinking and talking about a topic can help you develop your own ideas on the subject before you become influenced by the ideas you read about. It can help you to organise your ideas and information in a logical pattern. It can also mean that when you start reading, you approach the text with some ideas already in your head. This can help with comprehension of the text.

5.1b For the example essay plan, you can help students to think about the topic more thoroughly by referring them to the following article in the online *Guardian* newspaper:

http://www.guardian.co.uk/world/2007/nov/30/hacking.jamessturcke

This article helps to set the scene and also illustrates problems associated with hacking. It will help with students' brainstorming.

5.2 Encourage students to collect ideas from the text in the Student's Book and any other source, including the article from the *Guardian* mentioned above. The problem-solving framework can be used for putting the notes into various categories so that the ideas can be reused appropriately at the different stages of the essay.

6 Grammar in context: cohesive devices

6.1a Explain to students that referring expressions are used to allow writers to refer back to something that has already been mentioned, without the need to reuse exactly the same lengthy language.

> 2 hackers
> 3 limits
> 4 computer systems of organisations
> 5 unauthorized access (visiting computer systems without permission)
> 6 unauthorized access
> 7 crackers
> 8 footprints
> 9 thousands

6.1b For further guidance on anaphoric and cataphoric referencing, look at the two pages from the British Council's TeachingEnglish website:

http://www.teachingenglish.org.uk/think/knowledge-wiki/cataphoric-reference

http://www.teachingenglish.org.uk/think/knowledge-wiki/anaphoric-reference

> 3 forward   4 forward   5 forward   6 back
> 7 back   8 back and forward   9 forward

6.1c
> 1 a   2 b   3 b   4 a

6.1d Referring expressions are used to avoid repetition of complete noun phrases, which would be awkward. More importantly, they create links between ideas within sentences and between sentences. When a text contains clear links of this nature, we say it is *cohesive*.

Pronouns	they, it
Determiners	the, this, these, other

6.2 Check that students have grasped the differences between anaphoric (past) and cataphoric (future) referencing. As in the Student's Book, it is not necessary to use the technical terms, provided that students have followed the meaning and function.

> (Referring expression underlined; referent in italics; arrows show direction of reference.)
>
> The greatest *concern* is that many of the millions
> →   →
> of *internet sites* can easily be attacked by crackers.
>
> As a result, *crackers* have attacked more sites than
>
> ever. They substitute *images and words* on home
>   ←
> pages with ones that are embarrassing to the
>   ←   →
> *organization*. Almost 90% of existing Web sites
>
> have been victims of these destructive *changes*
>   →
> known as 'Web site defacement'.
>
> These *criminals* also break into systems and steal
> →
> personal information that can be used for identity
>
> theft. College students gain access to campus
>
> computers to charge books, food, and services to
>
> the accounts of other students. The *range* of
>   →
> reasons for unlawful entry is as varied as the
>   →
> Internet's *Web sites*.

6.3

2 the	**7** the	**12** It	**16** the
3 the	**8** This	**13** some	**17** This
4 other	**9** these	**14** the	**18** some
5 they	**10** their	**15** the	**19** their
6 they	**11** ones		

7 In-text referencing

7.1 If students are unfamiliar with the procedures for in-text referencing, guide them by telling them that they are looking for a name and a date. Even if some students are not yet familiar with the process, you should still be able to draw on the knowledge of the rest of the class from the other units in this book or previous experience.

> Long & Long, 2005

7.2   **1** C   **2** A   **3** B

7.3
> **1** ✓
> **2** Long and Long (2005: ~~301~~) make a distinction between hackers, who do not want to create problems, and crackers, who aim to cause harm.
> **3** Long and Long suggest that hackers present a legal challenge for countries around the world who 'are struggling to define suitable punishment to cybercrimes' (2005: **301**).
> **4** Long and Long (2005: ~~301~~) explain how the legal system dealt with the problem in the US in 1994 with the introduction of the Computer Abuse Amendment Act:
> This law changed the standard for criminal prosecution from "intent" to "reckless disregard", and it increased the chances of successful prosecution of two particular crackers (**Long & Long, 2005: 301**).
> **5** ✓

7.4 Students brainstorm ideas relevant to the essay title. If students have difficulty in coming up with ideas, remind them of the issues discussed in the texts in **2.2** and **5.2** to elicit ideas, e.g. computer viruses, hacking, cracking, identity theft, spam and phishing. Encourage students to reflect on their own experiences.

> **b** See the model answer on page 92.

Grammar and vocabulary

- Subordination
- Crime vocabulary
- Hedging language
- Cohesion

1 Subordination

1.1 It may be useful to help explain subordinate clauses by saying that they are clauses that cannot be used on their own in a sentence. Subordinate clauses have to be used with a main clause that they modify. For example: *Paul raised his hand in class **when it was his group's turn to answer the question***.

> **1** clause 1: the increase in computer crime
>   clause 2: it
> **2** is
> **3** clause 2
> **4** clause 1
> **5** when

1.2 👥 This exercise should help students to demonstrate their understanding of different types of clause. Ask them to work in pairs to complete the summary and then to check their answers with other pairs.

> **1** dependent   **2** *when*   **3** second   **4** sentence

1.3
> **a** Subordinators in **bold**, main clauses underlined
> **1** **While** most of us typically associate computer crime with the theft of sensitive data, <u>other less dramatic activities such as copying a music CD are also computer crimes</u>.
> **2** **Once** these controls were put in place, <u>business-related computer crime began to decrease</u>.
> **3** **Although** it is well known that computer crime is common, <u>no one really knows exactly how much is committed</u> **because** much of it is either undetected or unreported.
> **b 1** because   **2** once   **3** while, although

> **Optional extension**
>
> For additional resources for learning subordinators such as adverbs, encourage students to look at the English Page website at the following link:
> http://www.englishpage.com/grammar/Adverbs

1.4   **1** e   **2** d   **3** a   **4** c   **5** b

2 Crime vocabulary

2.1 This exercise helps students to understand nuances of meaning within a particular topic. It is also a good opportunity to demonstrate the power of dictionary use, as examples and contextual pointers can often be identified in example sentences.

1 *Theft* is a very general word that means 'to steal something from someone' and can be used for very small crimes like shoplifting; *robbery* is normally associated with more serious stealing from somewhere like a bank, and it can collocate with the word *armed*.
2 *Fraud* has a more specific meaning of trying to get money by deceiving someone.
3 A *prosecutor* works for the government (or the Crown in the United Kingdom and many Commonwealth countries).
4 in a court of law
5 *Do* is incorrect.
6 b (The phrase *criminal justice system* describes the process of judging people for crimes they have committed in a court of law.)

2.2

1 ~~come~~ go	2 ~~at~~ in	3 ~~robbery~~ theft
4 ~~from~~ by	5 ~~by~~ of	6 ~~makes~~ commits

3 Hedging language

For the exercises that follow, refer students back to the Student's Book on the work on hedging and check that they remember the concept and its purpose.

3.1 Incorrect examples:
1 frequently   2 By the way   3 must
4 It is generally spoken   5 In the end

3.2
1 could
2 probably
3 In most cases
4 Broadly speaking
5 It is generally agreed

Refer students back to the online list of grammatical categories mentioned earlier in the unit if they need further help with understanding grammatical terminology and its function.

3.3
1 <u>It is generally agreed</u> that the worlds of business and finance rely heavily on IT.
2 <u>In most cases</u>, small-sized businesses believe that computers have made their firms more efficient.
3 In the future, IT is <u>probably</u> going to become even more sophisticated.
4 Too much technology <u>could</u> result in a lack of human interaction in business dealings.
5 <u>Broadly speaking</u>, the business world is quick to take advantage of new technology.

4 Cohesion

4.1 Exercises in this section build on the work on anaphoric and cataphoric referencing. If necessary, check that students still understand the rules as described earlier in this unit.

1 main reasons
2 industrial espionage
3 secret lives
4 intellectual property
5 most companies'
6 finding out about intellectual property
7 most companies
8 competitor companies
9 a company's
10 a company
11 operation systems
12 a company's

4.2
1 Their   2 This   3 They   4 They   5 It
6 they   7 some   8 This

7.4 Model answer

Illegal or unethical computer use can also take place in universities. Hackers can access the websites of different university departments and change information about courses and staff. A student who wants to keep a library book for an extended time can hack into the library website and delete requests for the book from other students. Long and Long (2005) also note that hackers can charge purchases of materials and services to accounts that belong to other students. Finally, it might also be possible for a student to hack into a department's website and change their test results or grades and those of other students. There is a great variety of ways that illegal computer use in universities can have a negative effect on honest students.

10 Culture shock

Unit aims

READING
- Text organisation 3
- Grammar in context: reduced relative clauses

WRITING
- Planning the overall shape of an essay
- Reading for relevant information
- Writing the conclusion
- Creating a bibliography

LISTENING AND SPEAKING
- Concluding a presentation

Getting started

1 Cultural misunderstandings

1.1 As preparation for this activity, ask students to refer back to personal experience where they may have encountered difficulties caused by cultural misunderstandings. You can suggest categories if students are struggling. This might include matters such as gesture, personal space, gift-giving and forms of address. A useful framework to encourage students to think about might be a home-stay experience or time spent studying overseas.

1.2 👥 While the groups are working on their texts, go round and check that they have grasped the cultural misunderstandings which are illustrated in each text.

> Texts A and B refer to linguistic misunderstandings, while Text C refers to body language.

1.3 **a** Text C is different, as it resulted from an offensive gesture, not a language mistake.

Reading

2 Text organisation 3

2.1a In this section, students will discuss culture shock and choose an appropriate definition. To focus them on this topic, ask them what they think culture shock is and if they can give examples of what might happen when people experience culture shock. You might expect them to list some of the following:

People feel stressed or sick.

People miss home.

People get angry about certain cultural features or practices.

People adapt.

> Definition 2 is correct.
> Definition 1 is for the word *disarray*.

2.1b Encourage students to think about their initial experiences of a foreign culture. If they don't feel that they have really been culture shocked, you can still ask them to describe cultural features that they took time to get used to.

2.2a In a global business environment, a key focus of human resource management in multinational companies is the issue of culture shock. Discuss this issue and then summarise and evaluate ways in which human resource managers can deal with it.

2.2b Ask students to try and think of possible solutions to some of the problems associated with culture shock, as listed above. Try to draw on strategies which students may have practised or experienced.

2.3 Ask students to think about processes which they may have experienced, or accounts from friends and colleagues which may be relevant. This type of work is likely to result in students providing a series of anecdotes which are likely to be both interesting and worthwhile oral language practice. If very few students have experience of being or living overseas, ask the group to complete the question from a hypothetical position.

> **a+b**
> Diagram 2 is correct and is described in the text.

2.4 👥 If you have a dictionary to hand, weaker students can use it to look up the words in bold in order to help match the definitions to the vocabulary. Ask students to work in pairs and to agree on their answers before making their final decisions.

> **1** c **2** h **3** a **4** f **5** b **6** g **7** e **8** d

2.5 If necessary, in preparation for this exercise, it may be useful to look back at previous units where note-taking strategies have been introduced.

a Structure 2 is more appropriate for this kind of text, as it classifies different categories (in this case, the stages) of culture shock.

b Suggested notes:
overview: expatriates feel anxious / confused because environment & social customs are unfamiliar → happens in four stages
stage 1: honeymoon = optimism & happiness with new country
stage 2: culture shock = daily life (transport, school, etc.) creates stress → dislike of country & no connection
stage 3: adjustment = expatriate deals with new country → more positive & confident – ? more productive
stage 4: mastery = expatriate feels at home, but continuing need to learn

c The information will go in the early stages of the essay where key terms and concepts are being defined and described.

3 Grammar in context: reduced relative clauses

3.1a This work builds on activities in previous units relating to clauses. Explain to students that relative pronouns connect. There are numerous additional worksheets available on the Internet which focus on relative clauses. You can even demonstrate this to students by typing 'relative clauses' into a search engine.

> Examples a) and b) contain relative pronouns, while the versions in the text do not. Both versions are correct.

3.1b Ask students to work in small groups for this activity and to really study the two sentences to find similarities and differences. Remind them to look at both form and meaning.

> **1** Yes, the meaning is similar.
> **2** Example a) = cause   Example b) = find
> **3** *Expatriates* is the subject in example b), while *which* is the subject in example a).
> **4** yes, in both examples

3.1c Work on the active and passive voices is revised in this activity. Students can look back at previous units if they need to be reminded of the rules of usage and function of passives.

> **1** passive
> **2** the relative pronoun *which* and *is* (the *be* auxiliary of the passive)
> **3** active
> **4** The relative pronoun *which* has been taken away and the verb has been changed to an *-ing* (present participle) form.

3.1d This activity on relative pronouns can usefully be divided and allocated to different groups. Give groups a fixed amount of time and inform them that they will have to present their answers back to the rest of the class.

> **1** However, people <u>living</u> and <u>working</u> abroad for a long period of time go through the different steps of adjustment.
> **2** After that, in the second stage <u>known</u> as *culture shock*, expatriates begin to experience difficulties <u>connected</u> to their daily routines.
> **3** Next, in the third stage <u>called</u> *adjustment*, …
>
> Rewritten sentences:
> However, people <u>who live and work</u> abroad for a long period of time go through the different steps of adjustment.
> After that, in the second stage, <u>which is known</u> as *culture shock*, expatriates begin to experience difficulties <u>which are connected</u> to their daily routines.
> Next, in the third stage, <u>which is called</u> *adjustment*, …

3.2a Books closed. Before drawing students' attention to the activity, which requires them to select the correct options to complete the rule for relative clauses and pronouns, ask them to use their existing knowledge to write a rule of their own. When the rules have been presented to the class and discussed, then ask students to choose the correct options.

> **1** shortened   **2** subject   **3** *-ing*   **4** past
> **5** written   **6** reduced

3.2b Before starting this task, make sure students understand what a reduced relative clause is. A simple way to explain it is to tell them that a reduced relative clause is one that is not marked by *which* or *that*.

> **1** The honeymoon phase, **beginning** when the expatriate first arrives, can be a time of great excitement.
> **2** The feeling of excitement **felt** by new arrivals soon disappears.
> **3** Expatriates **trying** to adjust need a lot of support.
> **4** *No change possible – the relative pronoun is the object of the relative clause.*
> **5** The stress **created** by poor language ability can be the most significant problem for expatriates to overcome.
> **6** *No change possible – the relative pronoun is the object of the relative clause.*

Writing

4 Planning the overall shape of an essay

4.1 👥 Ask students to discuss their views in pairs, before deciding on an answer.

> **1** The flow of the plan is logical. Refer students back to the model essay structure types which have been mentioned during the course of the book.
>
> **2** In the body of the essay, Konrad is following a problem–solution text pattern.

4.2 👥 / 👥👥 Ask students to work in pairs or threes to identify the best introduction and to list the reasons why one of the introductions is superior, while the other is inferior.

> Introduction 1 is not suitable for the following reasons:
> - The broader context of multinational companies is not introduced early enough.
> - The definition of culture shock contains too much detail.
> - The example of the businessman is too detailed and should be included in the body.
> - The connection between language problems, company income and staff productivity is not coherent.
> - The role of human resource managers is vague.
> - The mention of staff families comes late in the introduction.
> - The mention of language training is too specific.
> - Coherent links are not made between the key problem of the essay and human resource management and training (i.e. that the latter is a potential solution to the problem).

4.3 Before completing this exercise, ask students, as a class, to describe the features of a good introduction based on their existing knowledge. Write down the suggestions made on the board. This will act as a useful springboard for the next activity.

> **1** a   **2** b   **3** a   **4** b

4.4 Once **4.3** has been completed and whilst the boardwork activity is still visible, ask students to think of a series of rules for writing an introduction. You could even ask the class to divide into pairs and solicit two or more rules from each pair. This will show that they actually have a good idea of the rules from their current knowledge and may help in completing the exercise which follows, where a set of the rules needs to be completed.

> **2** context   **3** key   **4** position
> **5** organised   **6** hang / cohere

> **Optional extension**
>
> Below are notes for an introduction to an essay, which discusses the different ways that multinational companies can staff new operations in foreign countries. Use the notes to write a complete introduction. Note that the word *staff* can be both a noun and a verb.
>
> – important consideration: multinational company (MNC) staff in new market
> – balance between central office staff & local staff
> – polycentric staffing approach = local staff in key positions
> – local staff = key benefit: local knowledge in new market → MNC gets ahead
> – essay: discuss different approaches → outline benefits of local staff
>
> See the model answer on page 100.

4.5 Once students have had a chance to compare their own versions in pairs, get feedback from the whole class. How did their examples compare with the examples in **4.2**? What did students change to improve their own versions? How well did they follow the rules in **4.4**? Students could also compare their own versions with the model answer on page 100.

5 Reading for relevant information

5.1
> **Optional lead-in**
>
> Check that students understand the difference between skimming and scanning. It may be useful to go through the following summary with them:
>
> **Skimming (for gist purposes)**
> Skimming is a way to quickly collect the most important details. Your eyes should quickly work through the text, focusing on key information. Use skimming to quickly grasp the main points being made. It's not necessary to be able to follow every word.
>
> **Scanning (for particular details)**
> We usually use scanning to identify a specific detail or element of information. Your eyes should move through the text searching for the particular detail or statistic that you need to find.

a Yes, the text would help Konrad.

b Summary 1 is better because it contains the key points from the main text. Summary 2 includes some unnecessary detail (e.g. the description of training activities), and it also suggests that these points should be included – something the original text doesn't say. In addition, summary 2 doesn't include the idea that host-country training is preferable, and the final comment about on-the-job training of managers is a detail from the original that doesn't link with the rest of the summary.

5.2 It may be useful to go back over the work on affixes done in earlier units if some students struggle to follow the aim of this task.

> **a 1** interpersonal
> **2** intercultural
> **3** host-country; in-country
> **4** multinational
> **5** senior-level
>
> **b** *inter* = between or among
> *host* = someone who welcomes visitors
> *in* = inside
> *multi* = many
> *senior* = older and therefore higher

Optional extension

PHOTOCOPIABLE

Prefixes and hyphenation in academic words page 124 (instructions page 109)

---

6 Writing the conclusion

Optional lead-in

Books closed. Encourage students to reflect on the structure of a good conclusion and to build up their suggestions on the board before starting the exercises in this section.

6.1
> **a** Correct order:
> **a** 5   **b** 2   **c** 6   **d** 1   **e** 3   **f** 4
>
> **b 1** To sum up   **2** In conclusion

6.2 This exercise should be facilitated by more boardwork and the Optional lead-in above. If necessary, refer students back to the boardwork, which will encompass reference to the structure of conclusions.

> Useful: 1, 4, 5   Not useful: 2, 3

---

7 Creating a bibliography

7.1

Optional lead-in

👥 / 👥 Lead a brainstorming session where students are asked to think about what can be found in a bibliography and why. Divide students into pairs or small groups and ask them to write down as many ideas as they can. It may be more interesting to set a time limit and to create a competitive spirit by suggesting that the winning team will be the group with the most detailed correct ideas.

> **a** Caligiuri, Hyland, Joshi et al. = paper
> Deresky = book
> Osland and Bird = article
> **b 2** F (just the surname followed by the initials)
> **3** T
> **4** F (If referring to a complete book, it is not necessary to include page numbers.)
> **5** T
> **6** T
> **7** F (It is the other way round.)
> **8** T
> **9** F (They should be included after the volume and issue number.)
> **10** F (The names of the authors of the specific article in the book are given first.)
> **11** F (The name of the book is given in italics.)
> **12** T
> **13** T

7.2 Encourage students to follow the model for writing a bibliography as used in the book. Explain that there is a wide range of bibliographic conventions and that the most important thing to remember is to use the referencing style as preferred and described for the department or tutor that they are working with. It is often the case that different subject areas also have different preferences, so it is useful to check in advance if you have not been specifically told.

Andreason, A.W. (2008). Expatriate Adjustment of Spouses and Expatriate Managers: An Integrative Research Review. *International Journal of Management* 25(2), 382–395.

Caligiuri, P. M. (2000). The five personality characteristics as predictors of expatriate's[*] desire to terminate the assignment and supervisor-rated performance. *Personnel Psychology* 53(1), 67–88.

Fontaine, G. (1996). Social support and the challenges of international assignments: Implications for training. In Landis, D. & Bhagat, R. (eds.) *Handbook of intercultural training edition 2* (pp.264–281). Thousand Oaks: SAGE.

Mead, R. & Jones, C.J. (2002). Cross-Cultural Communication. In Gannon, M.J. & Newman, K.L. *The Blackwell Handbook of Cross-Cultural Management* (pp. 283–291). Oxford: Blackwell Publishers.

Phatak, A.V., Bhagat, R.S. & Kashlak, R.J. (2009). *International Management: Managing in a Diverse and Dynamic Global Environment (2nd edition)*. New York: McGraw Hill Irwin.

Rodrigues, C. (2009). *International management: a cultural approach*. Los Angeles: SAGE.

Language note
The book title is listed as: ... *of expatriate's desire* ... The correct grammatical form should be: ... *of expatriate**s**' desire* ...

Listening and speaking

8 Concluding a presentation

8.1 (�))**10.1** To focus students before listening, ask them to suggest some effective ways of dealing with culture shock.

Topic 3

8.2 (�))**10.1** Explain to students that the listening skill used for this activity is similar to the aural equivalent of scanning, as students are listening for specific information about particular topics mentioned.

> 1 Language training: ability to learn language should be taken into account
> 2 Cultural training: done on the job with trainer/assistant to help
> 3 Material benefits: offer good money and benefit package in order to make relocation worthwhile

8.3

Optional lead-in
As an introduction to this exercise on concluding presentations, ask students to describe their own experiences of delivering a presentation and ask them how they marked the end of their presentation.

> Correct order
> **1** indicate you want to finish → **2** repeat key points from the presentation → **3** make a final, general point → **4** thank the audience → **5** ask for questions or comments

8.4

a Step	Word/Expression
1 indicate	that brings me to the end of my presentation
2 repeat	I'd like to finish off by summarising the main points
3 general point	overall
4 thank	thank you all for listening
5 ask	we've got a couple of minutes for any questions

b Incorrect words/phrases:

1 finale	**2** redo	**3** complete
4 hearing	**5** a survey	

8.5

1 reviewing	**2** reiterate	**3** to sum up
4 listening	**5** a few	

8.6 If students are going to prepare their presentations in class, this activity will be suitable for pair or group work. If time, ask groups to give their presentations to their class. Gather peer feedback if appropriate. What features made the presentations successful? Were the ideas clearly presented? Did students follow the steps outlined in **8.3**?

Grammar and vocabulary

- Word building
- Reduced relative clauses
- Participle clauses
- Compound words

1 Word building

1.1 Remind students of work on base words in previous units and, if possible, extend the activity by drawing on base words which may be of particular relevance to your discussions in class.

> 2 attainment
> 3 unattainable
> 4 significance
> 5 adequately
> 6 inadequate

1.2 Before trying to complete the sentences in this exercise, ask students to look at the words which precede and follow the gap to identify what type of word is missing. The surrounding sentence structure and grammar should provide a number of hints as to what kind of word has been deleted.

> | 2 attainable | 5 signify | 8 readjust |
> | 3 inadequate | 6 attain | 9 adequately |
> | 4 adjustment | 7 significance | 10 attaining |

2 Reduced relative clauses

> **Optional lead-in**
>
> Refer students back to the patterns provided for creating reduced relative clauses. It may also be useful to remind students of what the terminology actually refers to, by using examples. In many cases, the terminology risks appearing more complicated than the reality. This can be overcome by referring to *which* and *that*, rather than focusing too much on complex terms such as 'relative pronoun'.

2.1
> 1 Homesickness, **felt** by the children of many expatriates, can create behavioural problems at school.
> 2 Many companies offer preparation programmes **made up** of lessons in both language and culture.
> 3 Expatriate communities **offering** support to newcomers can play an important role in helping people settle in to life in a new country.
> 4 Anxiety **caused** by living in a new country can lead to problems with drugs and alcohol.
> 5 Expatriates **making** an effort to adjust to different customs are usually successful in the end.

2.2 Encourage students, where possible, to explain why the incorrect sentences are wrong. This will help to show that students have internalised the rule.

> 1 Local people **working** for multinational companies sometimes resent the attention expatriates receive.
> 2 Cultural information learnt by expatriates prior to their departure for a new country helps them to settle in. ✓
> 3 Companies ~~which~~ investing in cultural training usually see the benefit of the expense.
> 4 A cultural guide written by someone who has experienced life as an expatriate can be an effective aid for new arrivals. ✓
> 5 A training programme **leading** to trouble-free relocation of employees and their families would be very difficult to design.

3 Participle clauses

3.1
> a Both are correct and have the same meaning.
>   1 in the dependent clause
>   2 *they*
>   3 No, it is not stated, but we infer that it is the same as the main clause: *future expatriates*.
> b a sentence 1
>   b adverb
> c It refers to the object. This makes the sentence incorrect.

3.2
> 1 T 2 T 3 F 4 T
> 5 T (It makes it more efficient.)

3.3
> 1 **Before** attending lectures, trainees should do some background reading of their own.
> 2 **While/After** making every effort, some expatriates never manage to learn the host-country language beyond basic survival level.
> 3 **When** meeting people from the new culture, expatriates should try to relax and behave naturally.
> 4 **After/While** spending time in a host country, expatriates usually become familiar with the most common local customs.
> 5 **After/While** feeling confused initially, many expatriates make great progress learning the language of the host country.

4 Compound words

4.1 Refer students back to work on affixes both in this unit and in previous units.

1 host family
2 in-built
3 interchangeable
4 multidisciplinary

4.2
1 multidisciplinary
2 in-built
3 interchangeable
4 host families

Model answer

4.4/4.5 Model answer

An important consideration for multinational companies is how they staff a new operation in a new market. They need to decide on the balance between staff who already work for the central office and staff who are nationals of the country the company wants to move into.

A polycentric staffing approach means hiring local staff to key positions in the new operation. This approach provides multinationals with the key benefit of vital local knowledge that will help them get ahead in the new market. This essay will discuss different approaches to staffing operations in new markets and outline the benefits of employing staff who live in the new market.

Lecture skills E

Optional lead-in

Before starting this unit, ask students to review the work which they completed for the previous unit. Divide students into pairs and ask for a summary of the language and topic explored.

Preparing for lectures

1 Discussion

1.1 👥 For each of the questions, ask for a volunteer to suggest an initial answer, then ask pairs to look for a more in-depth response.

> Suggested answers
> **1** Governments can invest in alternative clean sources of energy such as wind power. More controversially, governments may consider nuclear energy as an alternative to fossil-fuel energy. Governments might also raise taxes on products that contribute to global warming, e.g. a high sales tax on petrol and coal. Governments can also ensure that large forest areas that absorb CO_2 are not felled, and they can subsidise housing insulation costs for home owners.
> **2** Fossil-fuel alternatives: bio fuels (e.g. bio diesel derived from vegetable or animal fat), energy derived from waste products (ethanol), wind power, solar energy, hydro (water) power (but creating dams can ruin the environment), energy derived from ocean waves and currents, geothermal power
> Nuclear power is also an alternative, but a less popular one.

> **3** Conserve energy at home, e.g. turning off lights, appliances, etc. when not in use. Ensure homes are well insulated in the winter. Install eco-friendly heating systems, e.g. underfloor heating, heat pumps. Use cars as little as possible and use public transport. Use air transport as little as possible. Avoid buying products created from felled forests.

2 Vocabulary for the context

2.1 In earlier units, note-taking was covered, so refer students back to the strategies which were presented. Ask them to discuss with you some of the abbreviations and symbols that they commonly use in their own note-taking.

> **a** **1** per cent
> **2** multiply or times
> **3** square metres
> **4** hours per day
> **5** kilowatts
> **6** squared
> **b** **a** 2 **b** 3 **c** 1 **d** 6 **e** 5, 4
> **c** **1** square **2** multiply

Listening

3 Scan listening and interactive listening

3.1 📻 E.1 👥 Students complete this exercise in pairs and compare notes after they have finished. This will help them to check their answers and identify any mistakes.

> **a** Correct order:
> **a** 3 **b** 6 **c** 2 **d** 1 **e** 5 **f** 4
> **b** not mentioned:
> 4   twenty kilometres
> 9   four kilograms
> 13 five years

3.2 📻 E.1 This activity encourages students to formulate a reaction to information that they listen to in an interactive way. Certain model responses are provided, but ask students to suggest alternative ways of responding.

Language focus

4 Guessing the meaning of vocabulary

4.1 [E.2] During this activity, encourage students to work out, guess or discuss meanings with other students in the group. Explain that they will often encounter new words and that it is important to build strategies to work out meaning, so that they can continue reading and understanding. This will avoid situations where they have to stop and lose track.

Below are the correct answers. However, the aim of the task is for students to guess. These answers should therefore only be given once students have discussed their guesses.

> **a Extract 1**
> **1** b   **2** b
> **Extract 2**
> **1** b   **2** a   **3** b
> **b carbon footprint:** Someone's carbon footprint is a measurement of the amount of carbon dioxide that their activities produce. (*CALD*)
> **photovoltaic farming:** using large solar panels to produce (or 'farm') energy

---

Optional extension

`PHOTOCOPIABLE`

Guessing meaning page 125 (instructions page 109)

---

5 *If* structures 2

5.1 Explain to students that the *that* in the extract refers to producing energy from wind farming.

> **1** did   **2** gave   **3** did

5.2 [E.3]

> **b** Dr Hunt probably sees the situation as more imaginary in the first extract and more possible in the second extract.

5.3 As this activity deals with intonation and stress, it may be useful again to model the sentence so that students can hear the stress even more emphatically.

> Stressed syllables in **bold**
>
> if we **did that**   If we **ac**tually **did that**
>
> These are also the clauses said in a high tone, so intonation and stress combine. Also, the two structures mirror each other and express the same idea. Having 'interrupted' the idea with a previously mentioned idea (*giving up ten per cent of the country*), Dr Hunt picks up the initial thought again. This time, he adds (and stresses) the word **actually** to make the possibility seem more of a potential reality.

Follow-up

6 Discussion

6.1 Point out to students that what people generally think may differ from one person's individual opinion.

Encourage further discussion on the matter by dividing students into two groups and asking each group to suggest one key solution to the problems caused by global warming. Make sure that groups each choose different solutions.

Hold a debate in class and ask students to vote at the end for the solution which they thought was presented most persuasively.

7 Further listening

7.1 [E.4] Before students watch the extract, go through the table with them to ensure that they understand the vocabulary (e.g. *PV farm = photovoltaic farm*) and the units of measurement (e.g. *kWh/d = kilowatt hours per day, m^2 = square metres*).

Photocopiable activities: instructions

Academic orientation

1 Make copies of the handouts on page 110.

2 👥👥 Divide students into groups of three or four and give each group a copy of Handout 1 (the list of common problems faced by students at English-language universities). Ask the groups to discuss what advice they would give each student.

3 Monitor the groups, helping weaker groups in particular.

4 When students have finished their discussions, give each group a copy of Handout 2, which contains the 'answers' to these problems. Students should match up each problem with an appropriate answer. Note: You should emphasise that these answers are not 'final', but rather guidelines.

> Pedro **d**   Ivan **e**   Jawara **f**   Zvedza **a**
> Kyung-Min **b**   Shan **c**

Unit 1

1 Make copies of the handout on page 111.

2 👥 / 👥👥 Tell students that they are going to read customer reviews from a book website of six of the sources mentioned in **6.2**. Give each student a copy of the handout and ask them to work together to write the name of the correct source for each review.

3 If any of the pairs/groups find the activity difficult, provide guidance/clues, e.g.
Are any of the title's key words repeated?
Does the review talk about the type of text it relates to (e.g. book/journal)?

> **Optional extension**
>
> 👥👥 Students discuss which of the books, based on these reviews, they would be most interested in reading.

> 1 Book 3 (*Success with your education research project,* Sharp (2009))
> 2 Book 5 (*Learning for themselves: pathways to independence in the classroom,* Wilson and Murdoch (2009))
> 3 Book 2 (*The Kolb learning-style inventory,* Hay Resources Direct (2005))
> 4 Journal 6 (*Learning and teaching,* Berghahn Journals (2008))
> 5 Book 1 (*Learning: principles and applications,* Klein (2009))
> 6 Book 4 (*Perspectives on the nature of intellectual styles,* Zhang and Sternberg (2009))

Unit 2

Handout 1

1 Brainstorm with students the importance of identifying an essay title's key words. Ensure they know the difference between 'instruction words' and 'content words'.

2 👥👥 Put students into pairs. Make copies of the handouts on page 112 and give the relevant section of Handout 1 to each student. They should keep the handouts secret from each other. Student A reads out their first essay title. Student B should identify the instruction words (**bold**) and the content words (underlined). Student A then confirms. Student B then reads out their first essay title for Student A to analyse.

3 They continue with their second and third essay titles in the same way.

Handout 2

4 Give a copy of Handout 2 to each pair. If students are unfamiliar with the concept of a crossword, provide this definition: *a game in which you write words which are the answers to questions in an interlocking grid, putting one letter in each square.*

5 👥👥 Working together, the pairs should complete the crossword using the definitions given. The answers are all instruction words from the essay titles they have just discussed.

1 impact	**2** statement	**3** agree	**4** assess	
5 pros and cons	**6** outline	**7** to what extent		
8 why	**9** problems	**10** increased		
11 importance	**12** justify	**13** discuss		
14 in recent years				

Lecture skills A

1. Ask students how symbols can be useful in taking lecture notes. Elicit responses such as:
   - *They can save time.*
   - *They can help the organisation of notes.*
   - *They can better show the relationship between ideas.*

2. If students are unfamiliar with the symbols and abbreviations featured, go through them quickly to ensure they understand their meaning(s).

=	the same as, means, can be defined as
c.	circa, roughly, approximately
&	and
≠	different, not equal to
v.	very
↑	increase, go up
↓	decrease, go down
→	leads to, creates
???	indicate where student has to look up information after the lecture, perhaps because they didn't hear clearly
>	bigger than, better than
+	positive, plus
–	negative, minus

3. 👤 / 👥 Make copies of the handout on page 113 and give one to each student. Using the symbols and abbreviations at the top of the page, they should try and complete the notes so that they make sense. Having done this, they compare their answers with their partner's.

4. Give feedback, ensuring that students are clear how each symbol can be used.

   - Neoliberalism (NL) **=** economic system created by Milton Friedman in **c.**1970s.
   - NL **&** classical economics **v.** similar, although some of their policies are **≠**.
   - In 1970s, there was **↑** inflation but **↓** economic situation. Inflation **+** stagnation **=** stagflation.
   - NL was first applied in Chile/China **???**.
   - Many argue that NL is **>** Keynesianism as an economic system.
   - Although there are many **+**s and **–**s of NL, supporters argue that, overall, it is a superior system.

Unit 3

1. 👤 Make copies of the handout on page 114 and give one to each student, asking them to evaluate the quality of each internet source. If students have access to the Internet in the classroom, they could actually search the websites themselves. If not, they should use the clues in the titles and URLs.

2. 👥 Students discuss which of the websites would be most appropriate to use in the essay, and why. Depending on the level of the class, it may be a good idea to do an example with them – number 2 would be a good choice, as it is probably quite reliable because it is a university site, as shown by the *.edu* internet suffix.

3. Discuss with the class their general impression of the sources.

   Whilst there is no 'specific' answer to this task, you might raise some of these points in feedback.
   1. Perhaps a good starting point as a way into the topic, but there are questions as to how reliable a source Wikipedia is, since it is not academically verified.
   2. The *.edu* internet suffix indicates that this is a university website, and so the quality/nature of the information is more likely to be appropriate.
   3. May be a good general source of information (www.history.com is a well-known website), but possibly the information might not be as academic as desired.
   4. This is an Australian government website (as indicated by the suffix *.gov.au*), so while the information may be interesting in terms of seeing some of the secondary effects of the Great Depression, it may not be directly relevant.

5 See source 2.

6 If you look at the organisation which wrote this source (the Foundation for Economic Development), you will see that they have a very specific and particular economic viewpoint (i.e. they are extremist free market). Therefore, the information could be considered to be biased.

7 The source was written in 1932, very shortly after the Great Depression. The fact that it was written so close to the event means that although it might give a contemporary view of events, it may lack analysis. Historians often say that you have to wait at least 20 years after an event to analyse it properly.

8 very relevant to the essay title, and from an academic source

Unit 4

1 Make copies of the handout on page 115.

2 Explain to students that prepositional phrases of two, three and four words are relatively common in all academic disciplines, and that being able to use these phrases can help their writing sound more academic.

3 ⬤ Give each student a copy of the handout and ask them to complete the gaps with an appropriate prepositional phrase using *for* or *with*.

4 ⬤⬤ Students compare answers. Take class feedback.

Optional extension
⬤ Students choose three of the phrases which they think will be of most use to them, and write sentences linked to their academic field.

> **1** With the exception of
> **2** for use in
> **3** with reference to
> **4** With the development of
> **5** For example
> **6** For this reason
> **7** for the moment
> **8** With respect to; with respect to

Lecture skills B

1 Make copies of the handout on page 116 and cut each one into a set of 16 cards.

2 ⬤⬤ Divide students into pairs and give each pair a set of cards. They should arrange these cards face down on the table. Tell them that eight of the cards represent the first half of a sentence, and eight the second half. Note that the 'first half' cards are printed in bold and each contains one of the words presented in **6.1** (or a related word); the 'second half' cards are in italics.

3 In turn, students play the game of 'pairs' (also known as 'pelmanism') to match up the two halves of each sentence appropriately. If a student turns over a matching pair, they take the two cards and have another go. The player with the most correctly matched cards at the end is the winner.

Alternative (less preparation time)
1 Make copies of the handout on page 116 and cut each one into a set of 16 cards.
2 Give students one card each and ask them to find a student with the other half of their sentence by walking about the classroom and 'mingling'.
3 For classes with fewer than 16 students, ensure that the appropriate pairs of cards are handed out. Where there is an odd number of students, you should also take a card and participate. If there are more than 16 students, make more than one set of cards and hand out additional pairs.

> **Many people have the perception that** *this problem cannot be solved.*
> **This issue is not seen as being particularly important** *and, as a consequence, has not been well funded.*
> **I'm going to be looking at** *a range of different ways in which this problem has been tackled.*
> **To analyse this trend properly,** *it is necessary to dig deeper.*
> **Although Stoddart makes his argument passionately, for me,** *his evidence is unreliable and the quality of his data is poor.*
> **I would like to put forward my own research** *as evidence supporting this position.*
> **One of the main points** *to be considered is that of economics.*
> **My basic question** *is as follows: how do we avert catastrophe?*

Unit 5

1 Make copies of the handout on page 117 and give a copy to each student.

2 Explain the game as follows:

1 *I will describe an object or idea to you using the 'defining' language we have just looked at.*

2 *I will give you three clues. After each clue, you should write down what you think the object or idea is. If you think your previous guess was correct, write it again.*

3 *I will then tell you the answer. You get 3 points for a correct answer after the first clue, 2 points after the second and 1 point after the third.*

3 Do an example with the class, following the procedure above, but giving the answer and going through the clues straight afterwards.

Clue 1: This animal can be defined as a mammal.

Clue 2: It is also known, more specifically, as a canine.

Clue 3: It is described in many countries as 'man's best friend'.

Answer: dog

4 Read the definitions below (or have a more able student do so), allowing time for students to think and write their guesses.

5 👥 Ask students to think of a word and write three clues for it themselves. They should then read them to a partner, who guesses in the same way as above. This can be repeated as many times as you feel useful.

Definition 1

1 This object is also called, usually informally, 'a motor' or 'wheels'.

2 This object can be defined as a machine used for transportation, usually on roads.

3 This object is also known as an 'automobile'.

Answer: car

Definition 2

1 This building is called what it is because it comes from a Greek word meaning 'movement'.

2 This building is defined as a place where you can go to watch films.

3 In America, it is known as a 'movie theater'.

Answer: cinema

Definition 3

1 This object can be defined as the only celestial body that humans have been to.

2 This object is more formally known as the natural satellite of the Earth.

3 The same type of bodies seen orbiting round Mars, Jupiter, Saturn, etc. are also called the same thing.

Answer: moon

Definition 4

1 This term can be defined as the change, over time, of inherited traits found in populations.

2 In general terms, it can also be called 'biological development'.

3 Because this concept is disputed, particularly by a number of religious groups, it is considered controversial.

Answer: evolution

Unit 6

1 👤 Make copies of the handout on page 118 and give one to each student. Tell students (or ask them to decide) which of the statements is to be discussed and give them a few minutes to note down some ideas for and against the topic.

2 Clarify language as appropriate. Words which may need defining include:

- *home student*: a student who is studying at a university in the country they live in
- *subsidise*: to pay part of the cost of something
- *ID card*: an official card with your name and photograph or other information on it that you use to prove who you are
- *censor*: to remove anything offensive from books, films, etc., or to remove parts considered unsuitable from private letters, especially sent during war or from a prison
- *capital punishment*: punishment by death, as ordered by a legal system (source: *CALD*)

3 👥 Assign each student a role: one who agrees with the statement and one who disagrees. Their own 'opinion' on the subject does not matter. They should then discuss the topic, ensuring that they use as many examples of agreeing/disagreeing language as they can.

4 Repeat the task with a different statement as many times as desired.

Alternative (stronger / more argumentative groups)

In Step 3, do not assign a specific role to each student. Rather, when forming the pairs, try to ensure that students will have different opinions, in order to generate as much of the target language as possible.

Lecture skills C

1 Make copies of the handout on page 119 and cut them into Student A / Student B sections.

2 👤 Divide students into pairs and give each student a copy of the relevant section. Using a dictionary (online, print or electronic), students have five minutes to look up words which have the same root as the three words on their handout and add them to the mind maps. They should indicate on the diagram what word class it is (i.e. noun, verb, adjective or adverb). In each case, they should write the three words which they think are most common in academic English.

Note: The words do not necessarily need to be semantically linked, e.g. *responsible/respond*.

3 👥 Student A presents their first list of words (for *contribution*), explaining the meaning in each case. Student B then chooses two of the words, and tries to put them into a sentence. Student A clarifies whether they are correct or not. Students then repeat this process in turn for their other words. Monitor and check throughout that the words are being used correctly. Make a note of any words which are considered difficult or are commonly misused.

4 Clarify any general questions / points of difficulty with the whole class. You should make the point with some of the words (e.g. *response/respond* and *spectacular/speculate*) that although the forms have quite different meanings, they do share the same root.

> The most common words which students might identify are:
> *contribution*: contributor (n); contributory (adj); contributing (adj)
> *glamorous*: glamorisation (n); glamorise/glamorize (v); glamorously (adv)
> *responsible*: response (n); respond (v); responsibly (adv)
> *methodical*: methodology (n); methodological (adj); methodically (adv)
> *revolutionary*: revolution (n); revolutionary (n); revolt (v/n); revolutionise/revolutionize (v)
> *spectacular*: speculation (n); spectacle (n); speculate (v)

Unit 7

1 Make copies of the handouts on page 120 and cut them into the two parts as shown.

2 Present this sentence to the class, underlining words as shown.
We tend to think of innovation, especially technological breakthroughs, as the product of talented, individual inventors or dynamic firms, which stand out from ordinary, less visionary counterparts.

3 👥 Put students into groups and ask them to discuss what they think *breakthroughs* means.

Handout 1

4 After one minute, give a copy of Handout 1 to each group and ask them to decide on the best definition (a, b or c) in the context of the sentence.

> **BREAKTHROUGH**
> a *advance*: This is close in meaning and is appropriately academic.
> b *revolution*: This probably has too strong a meaning; a *revolution* is an extreme change.
> c *step forward*: This is close in meaning, but a single word is probably preferable to a two-word phrase like this.

Handout 2

5 👥 Give each group a copy of Handout 2 and, for each of the three words, ask students to a) match the synonyms to their definitions, then b) decide which of the synonyms best matches the word in the sentence. (Note: The synonyms were provided by Microsoft Word.)

6 Go through the words with the whole group, providing feedback as necessary.

> The synonym with the closest meaning is in bold.
> **DYNAMIC**
> **1c** *go-ahead:* **enthusiastic about using new products and modern methods of doing things**
> **2b** *lively:* having or showing a lot of energy and enthusiasm, or showing interesting and exciting thought
> **3a** *vigorous:* very forceful or energetic
> **FIRM**
> **1c** *company:* **an organisation which sells goods or services in order to make money**
> **2b** *multinational:* a large and powerful company that produces and sells goods or services in many different countries
> **3a** *organisation:* a group of people who work together in a structured way for a shared purpose
> **VISIONARY**
> **1a** *creative:* producing or using original and unusual ideas
> **2b** *far-sighted:* **having good judgment about what will be needed in the future and making wise decisions based on this**
> **3c** *imaginative:* good at producing ideas or things that are unusual or clever, or showing skill in inventing

> **Optional extension**
> Using a dictionary, students look up one word each and provide three definitions. They then give these definitions to their partner, who performs the same task as above.

Unit 8

1   Make copies of the handout on page 121 and cut them into Student A/Student B sections.

2   👥 Put students into pairs and give the appropriate section to each student. Ask them to tell you if any of the linking devices are unclear. If they are, try and elicit a definition from another student.

3   👤 Give students time (10–15 minutes) to plan a two- or three-minute presentation on one of the topics on their card, which refer back to what has been discussed earlier in the unit. If students find the topics too difficult, allow them to do some research online if possible.

4   👥 Student A gives their presentation. Student B should listen, and tick off all the linking words which they hear. Afterwards, Student B should indicate if they think any of the linking devices were used incorrectly. They then swap roles, and Student B gives their presentation.

5   👥 Together, the pairs should look at any of the linking devices they did not use, and think how they could have used them in their presentation. Alternatively, students could prepare another presentation on one of the other topics on their card, focusing specifically on these linkers.

Lecture skills D

Students often find it difficult to use appropriate language to talk about graphs. This activity is intended to help them develop this.

> **Optional lead-in**
>
> Depending on the level of the class and their understanding of the relevant key language, it may be useful to check the terminology used to describe different types of graphic before starting this activity. For example:
>
> · **bar graph**: a mathematical picture in which different amounts are represented by thin vertical or horizontal rectangles which have the same width but different heights or lengths
> · **line graph**: a picture which shows how two sets of information or variable amounts are related, usually by lines or curves
> · **scale**: a set of numbers, amounts, etc. used to measure or compare the level of something
> · **axis (pl. axes)**: the lines on a graph which show particular values (the horizontal line is called the x-axis, and the vertical line the y-axis)
> · **legend**: the information which explains the use of colour visuals within the graph
>
> (source: *CALD*)

> You might also discuss with students the best way to describe this kind of information, i.e. start with the most general kind of information (e.g. what type of graph it is, its title) before moving on to more micro-level information (e.g. the graph scale, where it peaks and troughs).

1   Make copies of the handout on page 122 and cut them into Student A/Student B sections.

2   Put students into pairs and give the appropriate section to each student. They should keep them secret from each other.

3   👥 Student A describes Figure 1 (the line graph) to Student B as accurately as possible. Student B should draw the graph on the blank version on their handout. Student B is allowed to ask as many questions as they like to find out more information, but is **not** permitted to look at Student A's graph. It **must** be done orally.

4   They then swap roles, so that Student B describes Figure 2 (the bar chart) to Student A, who draws it on their handout.

5   After each graph has been finished, students should compare them, and identify how the discussion process could be improved.

Unit 9

1   Brainstorm with the class what prefixes can be used to make negative words, i.e. *un-, im-, in-, il-, ir-* and *dis-*. Ask students whether there are rules for making such negative words in English (answer: not really – the words must be learned, although what 'feels' or 'sounds' right can be a useful initial guide).

2   👤 Make copies of the handout on page 123 and give one to each student. Ask them to look through the list of words and decide which of the two forms they think is the correct negative form of the word in bold.

3   👥 Students compare answers in pairs and agree upon their answer.

4   Go through the answers with the class.

5   👥 Student A asks Student B a question using one of the positive root words. Student B answers using the negative form (without looking at the handout).
For example:

Student A: *Is robbery legal in your country?*

Student B: *No, it's illegal.*

They then swap roles.

Note: The student asking the question should try and anticipate that the answer needs to be negative.

Adjectives: unauthorised, imbalanced, incomplete, dishonest, illegal, illicit, disloyal, immeasurable, unpopular, irregular, unreliable, intolerable
Nouns: inability, incoherence, incompatibility, unemployment
Verbs: disallow, disappear, uncouple, undo

Unit 10

1   Make copies of the handout on page 124 and give one copy to each student. They should write a tick (✔) or a cross (✗) in the appropriate cell of the table according to whether a compound word can be formed by combining the two parts; in the example, the word *interactive* exists, but *multi-active* and *socio-active* do not.

2   Students compare answers and make appropriate changes. To check their answers, students consult a print or electronic dictionary.

3   Students practise using these words by either having a conversation in which they must use one of the words every time they speak, or choosing four of the words and using them in subject-specific sentences.

Base word	inter-	multi-	socio-
active	✔	✗	✗
biology	✗	✗	✔
demographic	✗	✗	✔
dimensional	✗	✔	✗
disciplinary	✔	✔	✗
economic	✗	✗	✔
ethnic	✗	✔	✔
media	✗	✔	✗
national	✔	✔	✗
purpose	✗	✔	✗
racial	✔	✔	✗
section	✔	✗	✗

Language note

During this activity, it would be useful to tell students the rules for when compound words use hyphens and when they do not. Essentially, it is a question of usage rather than grammar: the more common it is, the more likely it is to lose its hyphen. So, for example, *interactive* is quite a common word and so is not hyphenated, whereas *inter-disciplinary* is less common. Sometimes a hyphen is used to clarify meaning/pronunciation (e.g. where two vowels are next to each other, as in *socio-economic*). Words from the list which are more likely to be hyphenated are: *socio-biology*; *socio-demographic*; *multi-dimensional*; *inter-/multi-disciplinary*; *socio-economic*; *multi-/socio-ethnic*; *multi-purpose*; *inter-/multi-racial*.

Lecture skills E

1   Make a copy of the handout on page 125 and cut it into 12 cards.

2   Tell students that this is a 'mingling' activity. Give them all one card and ask them to find their 'partner'. Half the class has sentences with an unfamiliar word in bold, the other half has definitions of those words.

3   For classes with fewer than 12 students, ensure that the appropriate pairs of cards are handed out. If there are more than 12 students, make more than one set of cards and hand out additional pairs. Where there is an odd number of students, you should also take a card and participate.

4   If students get stuck, clues are available (see below). Either you or a strong student will have these clues. The other students may ask for a clue if they really cannot find their partner.

5   When everyone has found their partner, ask for the sentence, then the word definition to be read out. The other students state whether they think they are a true match.

Clues

- *ecovore*: The suffix *-vore* relates to food or eating.
- *anthropocene*: The prefix *anthro-* relates to humans.
- *trashion*: The word is a mixture of *trash* and *fashion*.
- *PAYT*: The *P* stands for *pay*.
- *hypermiling*: The prefix *hyper-* means 'excessive' or 'a large amount'.
- *slow food*: The phrase deliberately contradicts the more commonly used term *fast food*.

Optional extension

Students create new sentences (either orally or in writing) using the words in bold.

- **ecovore**: Someone whose eating habits are environmentally conscious
- **anthropocene**: The period from the 18th century until now, characterised by the increased impact of humans on the environment.
- **trashion**: Items and objects (especially clothes), considered fashionable, which are made from rubbish and recycled goods
- **PAYT**: 'Pay as You Throw' – a system where people pay according to how much rubbish they produce themselves
- **hypermiling**: Driving a vehicle in a way that reduces the amount of fuel which is used
- **slow food**: Food which is prepared in a traditional way using organic ingredients, which is better for health and the environment

Academic orientation

Discussing problems and identifying solutions

HANDOUT 1

Common problems faced by students at English-language universities

I'm finding it really difficult to locate the relevant texts in the library.

Pedro

I can't read all the books on my reading list. There are just too many.

Ivan

My tutor said that my vocabulary isn't academic enough.

Jawara

I don't understand anything the lecturer is saying.

Zvedza

My grammar is terrible, but I've no idea what to study to improve it.

Kyung-Min

I think I'm the only person on my course who's struggling.

Shan

HANDOUT 2

Match each of these responses to one of the problems on Handout 1.

a   Prepare well by looking at slides and doing the pre-reading. This will help in the lecture. Remember, you don't need to understand everything.

b   Look at your tutor's feedback for specific problem areas; think of your mother tongue and its specific differences with English.

c   This is probably not true. Talk to the other students on your course. They can be an excellent resource, e.g. in discussing lecture notes.

d   Ask a librarian for help; become more familiar with the computer system; ask other students for help.

e   Prioritise your reading list; learn to skim and scan more effectively.

f   Ensure you understand the difference between 'general English' and 'academic English'; keep a vocabulary diary as you read academic texts.

1 Styles of learning

Understanding book reviews

1

Research projects are carried out in schools and non-school settings by virtually all final-year undergraduates in the areas of teacher training, education studies and other educational contexts, and often in earlier years, too. Hot topics such as using the Net and plagiarism are covered, with up-to-date information, while key content on literature searches, critical thinking and the development of argument provide clear guidance and ensure academic rigour.

This is a review for _____

2

In a world of rapidly changing knowledge which requires new and transferable skills, classrooms are increasingly being viewed as places where pupils learn how to learn. In order to help pupils develop new skills, teachers must encourage them to work independently and manage themselves as learners.

This is a review for _____

3

One style doesn't fit all! Everyone has their own way of learning. Understanding your own style – and that of other people – can help you tune into the needs of others, so that you and your team work more effectively.

This is a review for _____

4

A peer-reviewed journal that uses the social sciences to reflect critically on learning and teaching in the changing context of higher education. The journal invites students and staff to explore their education practices in the light of changes in their institutions, national higher-education policies, the strategies of international agencies, and developments associated with the so-called international knowledge economy.

This is a review for _____

5

This text has received unending praise for its accessible and thorough coverage of both classic and current studies of animal and human research. Concepts and theories are introduced within the framework of highly effective pedagogical elements, such as chapter-opening vignettes, 'Before you go on' checkpoints, application boxes, chapter summaries and critical-thinking questions.

This is a review for _____

6

This stimulating and provocative text integrates the most recent theories and research on intellectual styles. The internationally acclaimed contributors address cutting-edge, controversial issues in the field that have yet to be resolved, including whether certain intellectual styles are better than others, how creativity affects intellectual style, and whether styles are traits or states.

This is a review for _____

2 Problems in the natural world

Instruction words and content words

HANDOUT 1

Student A
1 **Assess** the **impact** of climate change on the natural world.
2 **To what extent** do you **agree** with the following **statement**: The absence of honeybees from an ecosystem can have an extremely negative impact on human beings?
3 **Discuss** the **pros and cons** of alternative technologies.

Student B
1 **Outline** the **importance** of honeybees in the natural world.
2 **Why** have **problems** in the natural world **increased in recent years**?
3 **Justify** the introduction of a carbon tax for heavy polluters.

HANDOUT 2

ACROSS
2 Something that someone says or writes officially, or an action done to express an opinion (9)
4 To judge or decide the amount, value, quality or importance of something (6)
5 Arguments in favour and against (4-3-4)
7 The degree to which (2-4-6)
9 Situations, people or things that need attention and need to be dealt with or solved (8)
11 The quality of being important (10)
13 To talk or write about a subject in detail, especially considering different ideas and opinions related to it (7)
14 Recently, not long ago (2-6-5)

DOWN
1 A powerful effect that something, especially something new, has on a situation or person (6)
3 To have the same opinion, or to accept a suggestion or idea (5)
6 To give the main facts about something (7)
8 For what reason (3)
10 Became larger in amount or size (9)
12 To give or to be a good reason for (7)

Lecture skills A

Using symbols in note-taking

Use appropriate note-taking symbols or abbreviations from this box to complete the notes below.

=	???	↑	c.	+	↓
≠	>	⟶	&	v.	−

- Neoliberalism (NL) _____ economic system created by Milton Friedman in _____ 1970s.
- NL _____ classical economics _____ similar, although some of their policies are _____ .
- In 1970s, there was _____ inflation, but _____ economic situation. Inflation _____ stagnation _____ stagflation.
- NL was first applied in Chile/China _____ .
- Many argue that NL is _____ Keynesianism as an economic system.
- Although there are many _____ s and _____ s of NL, supporters argue that, overall, it is a superior system.

3 Indications and trends

Choosing internet sources

You have been given this essay title:

> *Outline factors that led to the Great Depression of the 1930s.*
> *Analyse what you believe were the main causes of this depression.*

A search for the term 'The Great Depression' on a well-known search engine returned this list of websites. With a partner, discuss which of these sources you would prioritise to start researching the above essay.

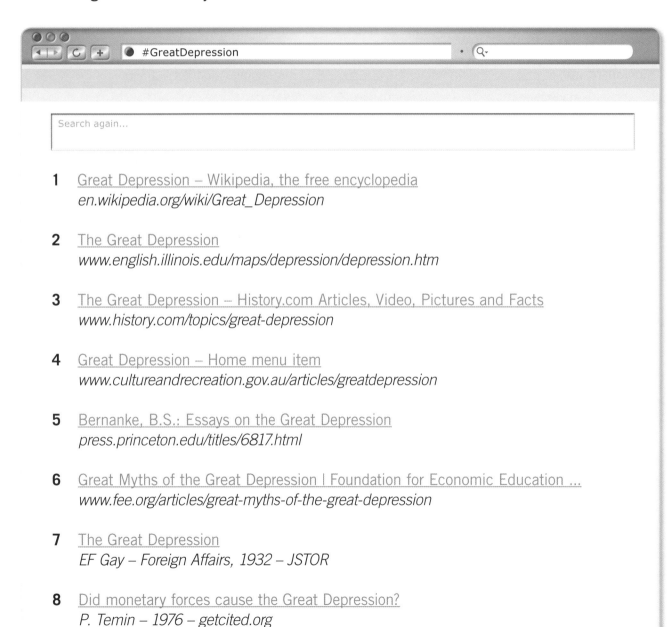

Search again...

1 Great Depression – Wikipedia, the free encyclopedia
   en.wikipedia.org/wiki/Great_Depression

2 The Great Depression
   www.english.illinois.edu/maps/depression/depression.htm

3 The Great Depression – History.com Articles, Video, Pictures and Facts
   www.history.com/topics/great-depression

4 Great Depression – Home menu item
   www.cultureandrecreation.gov.au/articles/greatdepression

5 Bernanke, B.S.: Essays on the Great Depression
   press.princeton.edu/titles/6817.html

6 Great Myths of the Great Depression | Foundation for Economic Education ...
   www.fee.org/articles/great-myths-of-the-great-depression

7 The Great Depression
   EF Gay – Foreign Affairs, 1932 – JSTOR

8 Did monetary forces cause the Great Depression?
   P. Temin – 1976 – getcited.org

4 The information age

Understanding prepositional phrases

Complete the gaps in the sentences below using one of these prepositional phrases, which are in common use in academic English. One phrase is used twice.

For prepositional phrases	*With* prepositional phrases
for example	with the exception of
for the moment	with reference to
for use in	with the development of
for this reason	with respect to

1 _____ a number of poorer countries, the majority of the world now has regular access to the Internet.

2 Ongoing improvements are being made in chip technology _____ PCs and laptops.

3 Fitzpatrick (2009) presents her findings about data usage _____ Pegler (2007) and Breen (2008).

4 _____ hardware capability, development in software capacity has also risen sharply.

5 There are many reasons why computers have revolutionised the world. _____ , people can communicate much more easily with one another.

6 Mobile phones have become an unignorable part of everyday life. _____ , many people suffer from anxiety when they lose their phone.

7 Governments are just about able to keep control of internet communications _____ , but this is likely to change as time goes on.

8 Information technology advances have created many advantages and disadvantages. _____ the former, there have been increased opportunities for friends and family to keep in touch with each other; _____ the latter, it has made it easier for criminal groups to coordinate activity.

Lecture skills B

Matching sentences

Many people have the perception that	*this problem cannot be solved.*
This issue is not seen as being particularly important	*and, as a consequence, has not been well funded.*
I'm going to be looking at	*a range of different ways in which this problem has been tackled.*
To analyse this trend properly,	*it is necessary to dig deeper.*
Although Stoddart makes his argument passionately, for me,	*his evidence is unreliable and the quality of his data is poor.*
I would like to put forward my own research	*as evidence supporting this position.*
One of the main points	*to be considered is that of economics.*
My basic question	*is as follows: how do we avert catastrophe?*

5 On budget

Guessing words through clues

Example definition	Guess	Points
after 1st clue		
after 2nd clue		
after 3rd clue		
Total		

Definition 1	Guess	Points
after 1st clue		
after 2nd clue		
after 3rd clue		
Total		

Definition 2	Guess	Points
after 1st clue		
after 2nd clue		
after 3rd clue		
Total		

Definition 3	Guess	Points
after 1st clue		
after 2nd clue		
after 3rd clue		
Total		

Definition 4	Guess	Points
after 1st clue		
after 2nd clue		
after 3rd clue		
Total		

6 Being objective

Discussing academic questions

Statements for discussion

Education

- It is right that foreign students are charged considerably more to go to university than home students.
- There should be no limit on the fees which universities can charge students.
- Governments should subsidise all higher education, since it is a way of investing in the future.

Politics

- International organisations such as the United Nations are ineffective at solving global problems.
- Democracy is the fairest and best political system in the world.
- People should be allowed to vote from the age of 16.

Privacy

- Every citizen of a country should be made to have an ID card.

Technology

- The Internet should be regulated and/or censored in order to protect people.

Language

- All education should take place in English, since it is the only true global language.

Law

- Capital punishment is an inappropriate punishment, and should not be allowable in any situation.

Generating new language

Student A

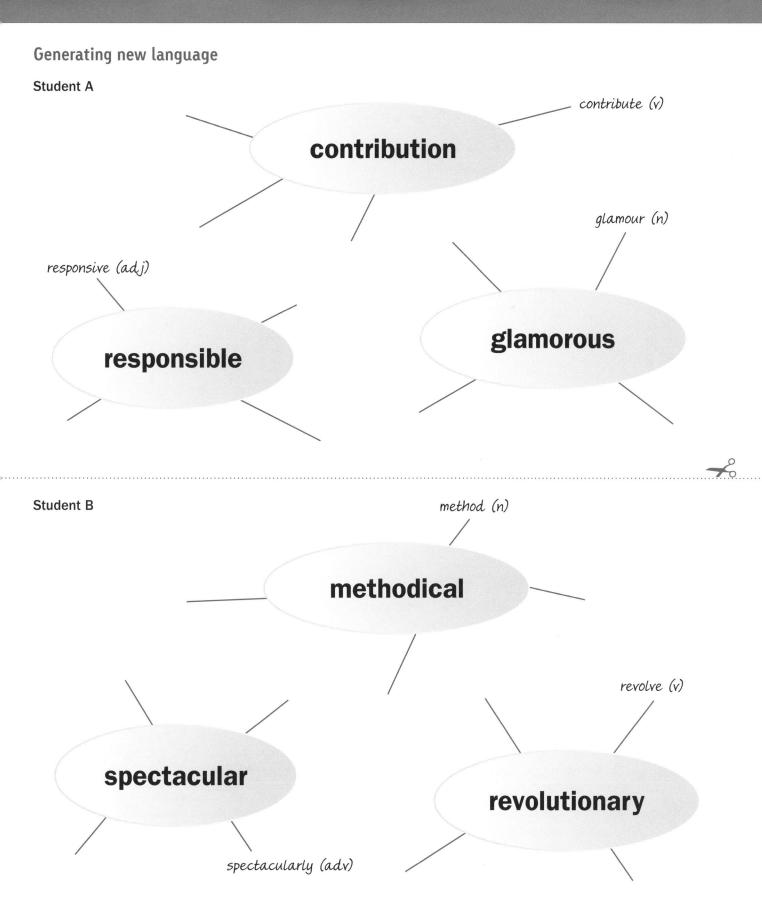

contribute (v)

contribution

glamour (n)

responsive (adj)

responsible

glamorous

Student B

method (n)

methodical

revolve (v)

spectacular

revolutionary

spectacularly (adv)

7 Innovation

Thinking about synonyms

HANDOUT 1

BREAKTHROUGH

a) *advance*

improvement or development in something

b) *revolution*

a very important change in the way that people do things

c) *step forward*

movement in the right direction

HANDOUT 2

DYNAMIC

1	*go-ahead*	**a)**	very forceful or energetic
2	*lively*	**b)**	having or showing a lot of energy and enthusiasm, or showing interesting and exciting thought
3	*vigorous*	**c)**	enthusiastic about using new products and modern methods of doing things

FIRM

1	*company*	**a)**	a group of people who work together in a structured way for a shared purpose
2	*multinational*	**b)**	a large and powerful company that produces and sells goods or services in many different countries
3	*organisation*	**c)**	an organisation which sells goods or services in order to make money

VISIONARY

1	*creative*	**a)**	producing or using original and unusual ideas
2	*far-sighted*	**b)**	having good judgment about what will be needed in the future and making wise decisions based on this
3	*imaginative*	**c)**	good at producing ideas or things that are unusual or clever, or showing skill in inventing

8 Sensing and understanding

An art presentation

Student A

1 Prepare a two- or three-minute presentation on one of these topics.

- The history of art in my country
- My favourite type of art
- Why art is considered important

2 Listen to Student B's presentation and tick all the linking devices you hear.

☐ First of all …	☐ I'd like to move on …	☐ If we now focus on this, …
☐ Having discussed …	☐ What I mean by doing this …	☐ Now we shall …
☐ Following this, …	☐ Returning to …	☐ After this, …
☐ Secondly, …	☐ If we now look at this, …	☐ During …
☐ Finally, …	☐ What I'm getting at …	☐ When …
☐ In addition, …		

✂

Student B

1 Prepare a two- or three-minute presentation on one of these topics.

- My favourite artist
- The importance of 'line' in art
- What is art?

2 Listen to Student A's presentation and tick all the linking devices you hear.

☐ First of all …	☐ I'd like to move on …	☐ If we now focus on this, …
☐ Having discussed …	☐ What I mean by doing this …	☐ Now we shall …
☐ Following this, …	☐ Returning to …	☐ After this, …
☐ Secondly, …	☐ If we now look at this, …	☐ During …
☐ Finally, …	☐ What I'm getting at …	☐ When …
☐ In addition, …		

Lecture skills D

Describing graphs

Student A

Figure 1: Share price of two companies in US dollars

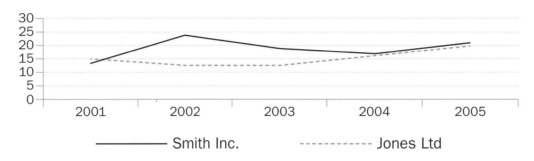

Figure 2: Election votes (in %) 1996–2011, Ruritania

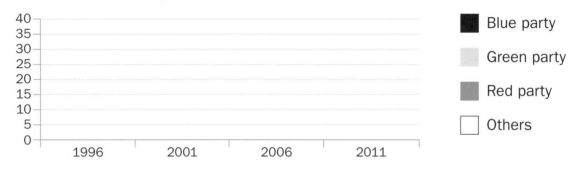

✂- -

Student B

Figure 1: Share price of two companies in US dollars

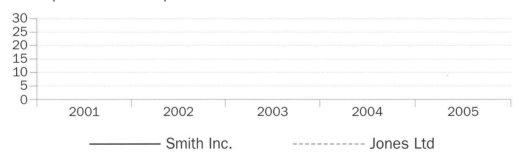

Figure 2: Election votes (in %) 1996–2011, Ruritania

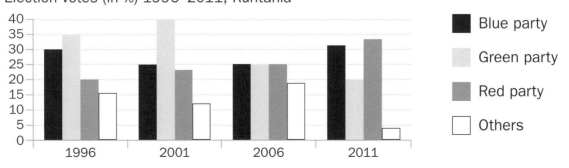

Negative prefixes

ADJECTIVES		
authorised	unauthorised	imauthorised
balanced	imbalanced	disbalanced
complete	uncomplete	incomplete
honest	imhonest	dishonest
legal	illegal	dislegal
licit	illicit	irlicit
loyal	unloyal	disloyal
measurable	inmeasurable	immeasurable
popular	unpopular	dispopular
regular	disregular	irregular
reliable	unreliable	irreliable
tolerable	distolerable	intolerable

NOUNS		
ability	irability	inability
coherence	incoherence	discoherence
compatibility	incompatibility	uncompatibility
employment	imemployment	unemployment

VERBS		
allow	disallow	unallow
appear	disappear	unappear
couple	incouple	uncouple
do	indo	undo

10 Culture shock

Prefixes and hyphenation in academic words

Base word	inter-	multi-	socio-
active	✓	✗	✗
biology			
demographic			
dimensional			
disciplinary			
economic			
ethnic			
media			
national			
purpose			
racial			
section			

Lecture skills E

Guessing meaning

One growing trend is for people to become **ecovores**, thereby avoiding any food which is detrimental to the environment, in order to ensure increased sustainability.	someone whose eating habits are environmentally conscious
During the **anthropocene**, carbon emissions have risen extremely sharply, largely as an effect of industrialisation and rapid population increase.	the period from the 18th century until now, characterised by the increased impact of humans on the environment
Trashion is a growing phenomenon, as designers seek to capitalise on people's interest in recycling.	items and objects (especially clothes), considered fashionable, which are made from rubbish and recycled goods
Many local councils are considering the implementation of a **PAYT** system for disposing of rubbish, rather than a 'one-price-fits-all' policy, meaning people would be charged according to the quantity of rubbish they throw away.	a system where people pay according to how much rubbish they produce themselves
Car drivers can save money by **hypermiling**, for example by slowing down their average speed, using an appropriate gear and maintaining tyre pressure.	driving a vehicle in a way that reduces the amount of fuel which is used
People think that they do not have time for eating properly in the modern world; one movement which is challenging this orthodoxy is called the '**slow food**' movement.	food which is prepared in a traditional way using organic ingredients, which is better for health and the environment

Photocopiable lecture slides

Economics and economy

What is Economics?

- ECONOMICS ...
- is the study of how society decides:

    - What
    - For whom
    - How

    to produce...

Resource allocation

Resource allocation is crucial for a society and is handled in different ways in different societies, e.g.:
- Command economy
- Mixed economy
- Free market

Photocopiable lecture slides

Women and the history of science

Hertha Ayrton (1854-1923)

I do not agree with sex being brought into science at all. The idea of 'woman and science' is completely irrelevant. Either a woman is a good scientist, or she is not.

Girton chemistry laboratory

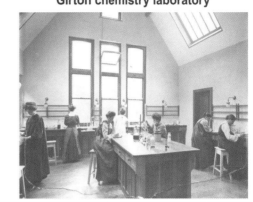

Hertha Ayrton (1854-1923)

- 1881 Gained a Certificate in Mathematics at Cambridge (Girton College)

- 1902 Proposed for Fellowship of the Royal Society

Mary Somerville

- 1826 paper in *Philosophical Transactions*

Antoine Lavoisier (1743-94)
Marie Paulze Lavoisier(1758-1836)

Photocopiable lecture slides

Women and the history of science

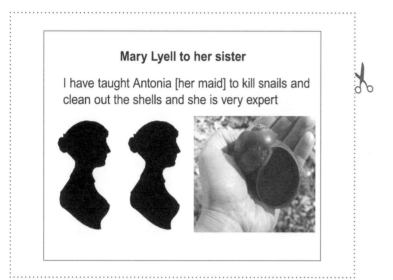

Photocopiable lecture slides

Climate change and sustainable energy

Questions:

1. Is climate change for real?

2. Should I be worried?

3. What are my own CO_2 emissions?

4. What can I do to make a difference?

What is the UK average CO_2 footprint?

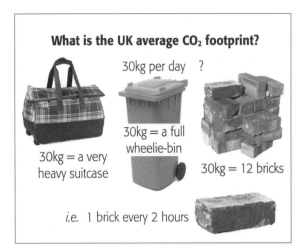

30kg per day ?

30kg = a very heavy suitcase

30kg = a full wheelie-bin

30kg = 12 bricks

i.e. 1 brick every 2 hours

The atmosphere is thin.

It contains 2,000,000,000,000,000 kg of CO_2

World population = 6,700,000,000

We produce 5,000 kg CO_2/person per year

(12,000 kg UK)

(25,000 kg USA)

ie 2,000,000,000,000,000 kg CO_2 in 60 years

We rely on trees and oceans to suck it all up

Something must be done!

LOVE HATE

Two reasons to join GREENPEACE

Cars

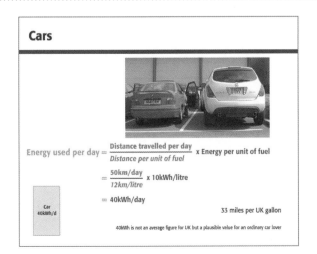

Energy used per day = $\dfrac{\text{Distance travelled per day}}{\textit{Distance per unit of fuel}}$ x Energy per unit of fuel

$= \dfrac{50km/day}{12km/litre}$ x 10kWh/litre

$= 40kWh/day$

33 miles per UK gallon

40kWh is not an average figure for UK but a plausible value for an ordinary car lover

Car 40kWh/d

Wind

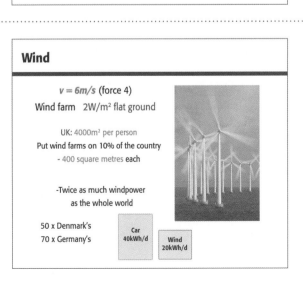

$v = 6m/s$ (force 4)

Wind farm   2W/m² flat ground

UK: 4000m² per person

Put wind farms on 10% of the country
- 400 square metres each

-Twice as much windpower
as the whole world

50 x Denmark's
70 x Germany's

Car 40kWh/d

Wind 20kWh/d

Photocopiable lecture slides

Climate change and sustainable energy

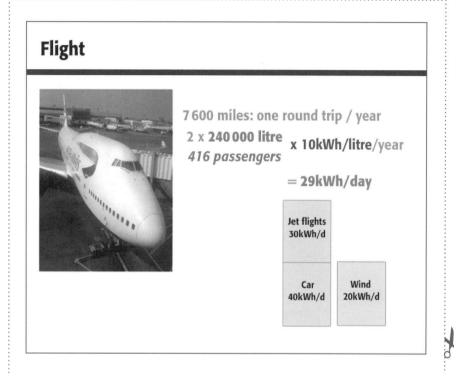

Flight

7 600 miles: one round trip / year

$2 \times \mathbf{240\,000\ litre}$ x 10kWh/litre/year

416 passengers

= **29kWh/day**

Jet flights 30kWh/d

Car 40kWh/d

Wind 20kWh/d

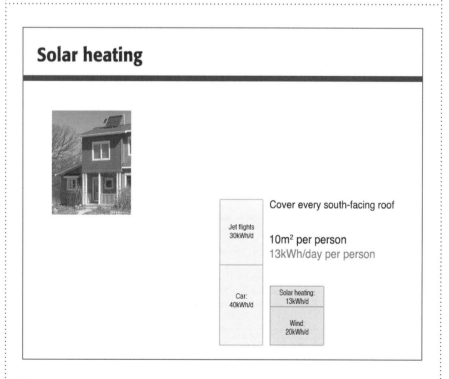

Solar heating

Cover every south-facing roof

10m² per person

13kWh/day per person

Jet flights 30kWh/d

Car: 40kWh/d

Solar heating: 13kWh/d

Wind: 20kWh/d

Photocopiable lecture slides

Climate change and sustainable energy

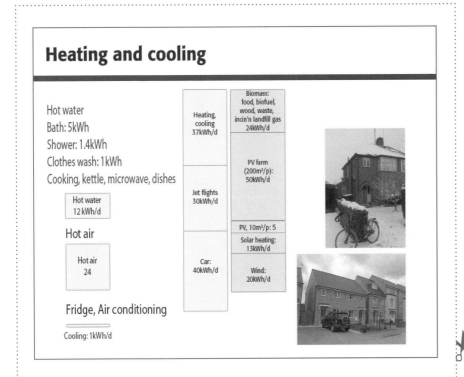

Heating and cooling

Hot water
Bath: 5kWh
Shower: 1.4kWh
Clothes wash: 1kWh
Cooking, kettle, microwave, dishes

Hot water
12 kWh/d

Hot air

Hot air
24

Fridge, Air conditioning

Cooling: 1kWh/d

Heating, cooling 37kWh/d

Jet flights 30kWh/d

Car: 40kWh/d

Biomass: food, biofuel, wood, waste, incin'n landfill gas 24kWh/d

PV farm (200m²/p): 50kWh/d

PV, 10m²/p: 5
Solar heating: 13kWh/d

Wind: 20kWh/d

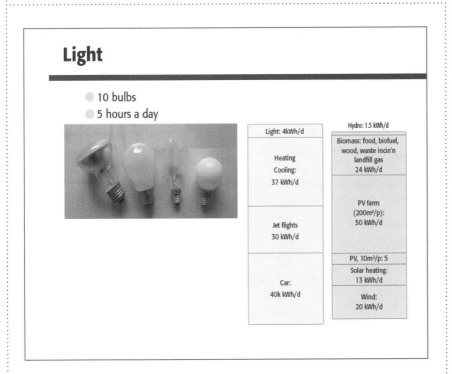

Light

- 10 bulbs
- 5 hours a day

Light: 4kWh/d

Heating Cooling: 37 kWh/d

Jet flights 30 kWh/d

Car: 40k kWh/d

Hydro: 1.5 kWh/d

Biomass: food, biofuel, wood, waste incin'n landfill gas 24 kWh/d

PV farm (200m²/p): 50 kWh/d

PV, 10m²/p: 5
Solar heating: 13 kWh/d

Wind: 20 kWh/d

Photocopiable lecture slides

Climate change and sustainable energy

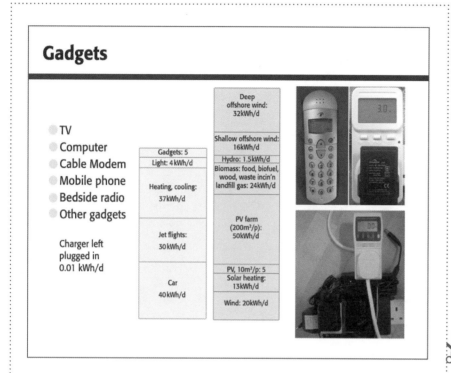

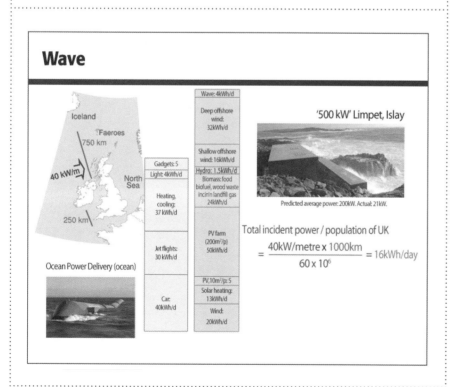

Climate change and sustainable energy

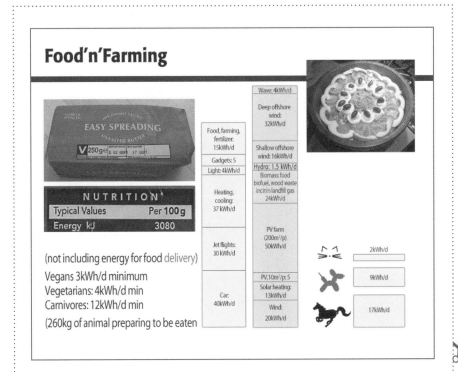

Food 'n' Farming

(not including energy for food delivery)

Vegans 3kWh/d minimum

Vegetarians: 4kWh/d min

Carnivores: 12kWh/d min

(260kg of animal preparing to be eaten

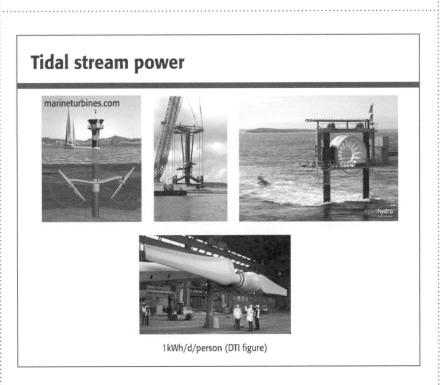

Tidal stream power

1kWh/d/person (DTI figure)

Photocopiable lecture slides

Climate change and sustainable energy

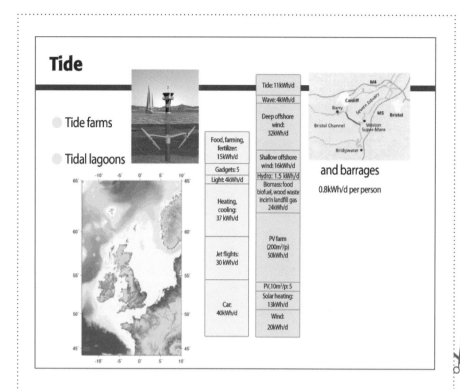

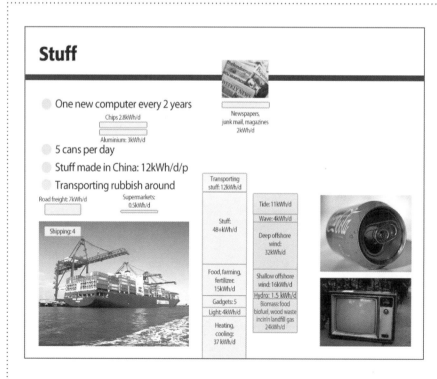

Climate change and sustainable energy

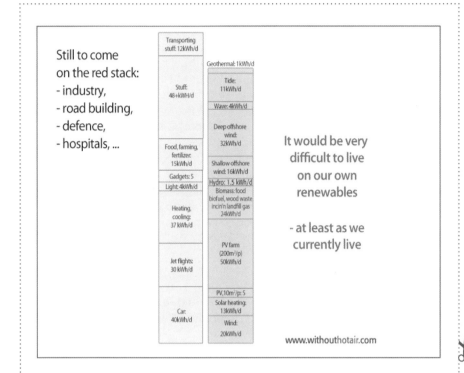

Acknowledgements

I would like to thank:

The team at Cambridge University Press for all their help and support. The staff and students of the University of Kent and the Centre for English and World Languages whose teaching context has provided useful inspiration for the guidance provided in this Teachers' Book. Amy and Imogen for their patience with me during the writing process.

Anthony Manning

Chris Sowton would like to thank Kate Hansford at Cambridge University Press and Catriona Watson-Brown for her editorial work.

Text and Photo Acknowledgements

The authors and publishers acknowledge the following sources of copyright material and are grateful for the permissions granted. While every effort has been made, it has not always been possible to identify the sources of all the material used, or to trace all copyright holders. If any omissions are brought to our notice, we will be happy to include the appropriate acknowledgements on reprinting.

The publisher has used its best endeavours to ensure that the URLs for external websites referred to in this book are correct and active at the time of going to press. However, the publisher has no responsibility for the websites and can make no guarantee that a site will remain live or that the content is or will remain appropriate.

Corpus

Development of this publication has made use of the Cambridge English Corpus (CEC). The CEC is a computer database of contemporary spoken and written English, which currently stands at over one billion words. It includes British English, American English and other varieties of English. It also includes the Cambridge Learner Corpus, developed in collaboration with the University of Cambridge ESOL Examinations. Cambridge University Press has built up the CEC to provide evidence about language use that helps to produce better language teaching materials.

CALD

The Cambridge Advanced Learner's Dictionary is the world's most widely used dictionary for learners of English. Including all the words and phrases that learners are likely to come across, it also has easy-to-understand definitions and example sentences to show how the word is used in context. The Cambridge Advanced Learner's Dictionary is available online at dictionary.cambridge.org. © Cambridge University Press, 2012, reproduced with permission.

Photo Acknowledgements

The publishers are grateful to the following for permission to reproduce copyright photographs and material on pages 126–135:

Key: l = left, c = centre, r = right, t = top, b = bottom

AKG-Images/©Erich Lessing for p127(br); Alamy/©Peter Bonek for p128(r); Cambridge University Library Syndics for p127(cl) – reproduced by kind permission; David Mackay for p129(bl), p130(t,b), p131(tr,cr,b), p132(tr,ct), p133(tl,tr), p134(c), p134(rt,rb); Fotolia/©Nigel Monckton for p129(tr); Getty Images/©Reinhold Thiele for p127(tr); Greenpeace for p129(c); Ian Boyle/©www.simplonpc.co.uk for p134(bl); istockphoto/©mattjeacock for p129(tc), /©Lars Lentz for p129(cl); Marine Current Turbines Ltd for p133(cl,cc,b), p134(tl); Open Hydro for p133(cr); Pelamis Wave Power - www.pelamiswave.com for p132(bl); Science Photo Library/©Emilio Segre Visual Archives/ American Institute of Physics for p127(tl), /©Omikron for p127(bl); Shutterstock/©Venue Angel for p129(tl); Voith Hydro Wavegen for p132(cb)); Wellcome Library, London for p127(cr, bc)

Text on slide images on page 126:
David Begg, Stanley Fischer and Rudiger Dornbusch, Economics, © 2002, Reproduced with kind permission of Open University Press

Slides on pages 129 to 135 for the *Climate Change and Sustainable Energy* lecture, delivered by Dr Hugh Hunt: adapted from *Sustainable Energy – without the hot air*, by David JC MacKay, published by UIT: www.uit.co.uk/ sustainable. Also available free to download for personal non-commercial use from www.withouthotair.com

Picture Research by Hilary Luckcock
Editing by Catriona Watson-Brown